SHAW'S GUIDE TO THE RENT ACT 1974

Shaw's Guide to
THE RENT ACT 1974

by

HUGH ROSSI, LL.B., M.P.

A Solicitor of the Supreme Court (Hons.)
(a former Parliamentary Under-Secretary
of State for the Environment)

———

LONDON:
Printed and Published by
SHAW & SONS LTD.,
Shaway House,
London, SE26 5AE
1974

Published - - - - *August,* 1974

ISBN 0 7219 0570 6

© SHAW & SONS Ltd. 1974.
Printed in Great Britain.

DEDICATION

This manual is dedicated to—

—my indefatigable colleagues James Allason, M.P.
Walter Clegg, M.P., Sir John Gilmour, M.P., Ivan Law-
rence, M.P., the Rt. Hon. R. Graham Page, M.P., W. R.
Rees-Davies, M.P., and Tim Sainsbury, M.P., who cheer-
fully sat with me through the small hours of the night to
probe and improve this measure

—and to my most patient wife and family who having
tolerated the unsocial hours of a Parliamentary session,
saw me emerge only to disappear into the confines of my
study.   But for their understanding this guide could never
have been produced.

H. R.

PREFACE

This small manual on the Rent Act 1974 was compiled immediately upon my emerging from the Report Stage in the Commons. Conscious of the great difficulties encountered during the passage of the Bill I felt that an explanatory note might be of help to the many practitioners and others who will have to contend with its provisions.

As the Act was due to come into force within two weeks of enactment speed in production was essential, and time has not permitted the inclusion of an index, but it is hoped the expanded table of contents will prove adequate for this purpose.

HUGH ROSSI, M.P.

House of Commons, S.W.1.
August 1974

TABLE OF CONTENTS

[i]

C.—TEXT OF THE RENT ACT 1974.

Modifications of Rent Act in relation to furnished and other tenancies

Furnished lettings (England and Wales)

Furnished lettings (Scotland)

Supplementary

SHAW'S GUIDE TO THE RENT ACT 1974

A.—GENERAL COMMENTARY

INTRODUCTION

The Rent Act 1974 received the Royal Assent on the 31st July 1974 and came into force within the remarkably short space of two weeks, namely on the 14th August 1974.

Its avowed political objective is " to give protection to the 750,000 furnished tenants who are at risk as to the security of their own homes " (Shelter). The figure of 750,000 derives from the total number of furnished tenancies given in the 1971 Census. However, the bland assertion is questionable since the Act in no way affects the unidentified number of furnished tenants living in the same building as their landlord (purpose built blocks of flats excluded).

Possibly a sounder way of testing the need for the Act is to examine the number of cases in which Rent Tribunals have found it necessary to grant a period of security to furnished tenants. This is on the assumption that the landlords of the 750,000 have let because they want to rent their property and not simply to enjoy the process of eviction. In an answer to my Parliamentary Question, an Under Secretary of State for the Environment on the 10th July 1974 gave figures to show that, over the past four years, on average 7,500 applications for security were granted each year by Rent Tribunals. This 7,500 includes second and third applications for extension of security, so that the number of furnished tenants " at risk " for the first time each year must be well below 1% of the alarming 750,000 posited.

It is also open to considerable doubt whether the Act was necessary since the recent decision of *Woodward v. Docherty* (*see below*).

However, a political pledge once given must be seen to be redeemed particularly in the run up to a general election. Hence, practitioners now have to contend with a measure prepared in unseemly haste and pressured through a Parliament

B

unable to give it due and proper consideration. Therefore, there need not be undue surprise if a few anomalies emerge. Nevertheless, there is no cause for despair since the Ministers in charge of the bill have undertaken to bring in remedial legislation sometime in the future!

Meanwhile, it is hoped that this brief guide may be of help to those who will have the unenviable task of picking their way through a short but complex statute incorporating many of the worst features of legislation by reference.

FURNISHED OR UNFURNISHED ?

The Act starts with the simple intent of removing the distinction between furnished and unfurnished accommodation. Thereby it aims to bring a substantial proportion of all furnished accommodation into the full protection hitherto only enjoyed in respect of unfurnished lettings.

It will be recalled that since the decision of *Sagoo v. Goel* [1969] 2 W.L.R., the commonly held view was that accommodation was " furnished " if it contained the essentials of a home irrespective of the arithmetical relationship of the rent of the furniture to the rent paid. This view was upset by the Court of Appeal in *Woodward v. Docherty* as recently as the 24th April 1974 when Scarman L.J. pronounced that " the judge below has attached too much importance to the fact that the flat was fully furnished ". It was held that the rent fairly attributable to the use of the furniture must be a substantial part of the rent. Hence to fill a flat with furniture readily and relatively cheaply available from a dealer would not make it furnished for the purpose of the Rent Act 1968.

This decision has the considerable practical effect of moving the barrier between furnished and unfurnished in favour of the tenant. In practice, the rent of a great many furnished lettings does not include a substantial payment for the use of furniture. This is particularly true of the area of furnished lettings which the Act was conceived to protect. That is to say, the young family in neighbourhoods of housing stress forced to make their permanent home in furnished accommodation, very often a mockery of that term, because there is nowhere else to live.

The Act therefore was anticipated and made unnecessary by the Courts but it has been brought forward to have some far-reaching and curious effects.

RESIDENT AND NON-RESIDENT LANDLORDS

Having nullified to all intents and purposes the distinction between furnished and unfurnished rented accommodation, the Act creates and imposes a new distinction. This distinction is between rented accommodation where the landlord resides in the same building as his tenants and where he does not.

Dependent on this residence of the landlord there are a number of consequences irrespective of whether the premises are let furnished or unfurnished. This residence will determine:—

(a) whether there is security of tenure in the full sense;

(b) whether the tenant makes his application to a rent officer or to the Rent Tribunal to fix his rent;

(c) whether the rent is to be a " fair rent " under section 46 of the Rent Act 1968 or a " rent reasonable in all the circumstances " under section 73 of the same Act.

Therefore, to take a hypothetical case it is possible for a man to own a pair of semi-detached houses which he converts into four flats living in one himself. The tenant in the same house as himself, if dissatisfied, can go to the Rent Tribunal to fix a reasonable rent and will have no security of tenure other than that given by the Tribunal; and even this is now non-existent in case of misbehaviour. The tenants next door in identical accommodation with identical furniture, if let furnished, go to the rent officer for a fair rent and enjoy the same full security extended by section 10 of the Rent Act 1968 as formerly enjoyed only in respect of unfurnished accommodation.

It is difficult to imagine any more absurd a legal situation. Two parallel administrative or quasi-judicial machinery applying separate criteria to establish the rents of what could be identical accommodation. One can only hope that the common-sense of rent officers and Rent Tribunals will ensure a co-ordination of approach that will not produce absurdly disparate results.

Certainly, the early fusion of these two systems must be expected. From the debate in the Commons Standing Committee this will be achieved by the abolition of the Rent Tribunals. Meanwhile, tenants accustomed to a four or five week wait for a Rent Tribunal to fix the rents will find themselves having to wait in some parts of London anything up to twelve months for overburdened rent officers' determinations. How this will help a furnished tenant believing he is overcharged, it is hard to see.

A particular trap for the unwary exists for practitioners creating trusts for sale as will be seen when we come to consider Schedule 2, Part II, and the effects of new section 5A (3).

Finally, it must be borne in mind that in respect of tenancies granted *before* the commencement of the Act, the distinction between unfurnished and furnished accommodation remains of relevance where there is a resident landlord. The former remain fully protected tenancies and the latter Part VI contracts under the Rent Act 1968. This is because only furnished lettings with non-resident landlords are carried into protection as a result of the combined effects of section 1 and Schedule 3 of the Act. Therefore *Woodward v. Docherty* is of considerable importance still in determining whether tenancies granted before the Act are protected or not where there is a resident landlord.

RATEABLE VALUE LIMITS

Prior to the Act, furnished lettings fell within the jurisdiction of the Rent Tribunal if the rateable value of the accommodation did not exceed £1,000 in Greater London and £500 outside. They have been now brought into line with unfurnished accommodation and the limits are £1,500 and £750 respectively. This means that furnished accommodation commanding up to £90 per week in rent in Inner London will be protected, and properties of up to a capital value of £35,000 outside.

TENANCIES NOT PROTECTED

Section 2 of the Rent Act 1968 will continue to apply to define those tenancies not subject to full rent control; except, of course, the effect of the Rent Act 1974 is to remove the provision of furniture as one of the exemptions.

The most important of the old exemptions is where the rent includes payment for board or attendance.

One can envisage a situation developing whereby non-resident landlords, who are those most affected by the Act, will enter into the business of providing breakfast for their tenants. No doubt the installation of a vending machine for hot morning coffee would not suffice. However, the incentive will be sufficiently large to see a room set aside in which a daily woman will come to prepare fresh tea or coffee every morning, a 6p boiled egg and some bread and toast. The loss of a room and the cost of the daily and the food and drink will be a small enough price to pay for ensuring vacant possession when required and no interference by rent officers. Again there will be agonising political re-appraisals of " evasions " and " abuse " by " unscrupulous landlords ".

To these existing exemptions, the 1974 Act adds three new categories in section 2 (below):—

(1) tenancies let by specified educational institutions to students but not by private non-resident landlords;
(2) lettings for the purpose of a holiday;
(3) lettings by resident landlords.

RECOVERY OF POSSESSION

Where the landlord is resident in the same building as his tenants, possession will be recovered by Court order based upon the expiration of a notice to quit. The Rent Tribunal may give security of tenure for limited periods under Part VI of the 1968 Rent Act. However, where the tenant does not pay his rent, damages the landlord's property (including the furniture), or acts in an anti-social manner, the landlord will be able to go direct to the County Court without being delayed by Rent Tribunal procedures.

Where the landlord is non-resident, section 10 and the 3rd Schedule of the Rent Act 1968 which stipulate when the Court may or must make an order for possession will apply.

The 1974 Act adds one new case to Part I of the 3rd Schedule of the 1968 Act, namely Case 3A where the tenant ill-treats the landlord's furniture. Here the power of the Court is discretionary.

The new Act also adds two new cases where the Court must make an order for possession—

(a) Case 10A (11A in Scotland) where the landlord has retired from regular employment and he requires possession of a dwelling he bought for his eventual retirement.

(b) Case 10B (11B in Scotland) where the landlord has let normal holiday accommodation out-of-season.

FIXED TERM LETTINGS

A common device used in the past to avoid the jurisdiction of Rent Tribunals in respect of furnished lettings was for a landlord to grant his tenant a succession of tenancies under agreements each for a fixed term. Since the security of tenure given by the Rent Tribunal was based upon the suspension of a notice to quit for stipulated periods, such security was avoided where a tenant could be made to vacate by effluxion of time without need to serve a notice.

This device can no longer be used.

Where the landlord is non-resident, all furnished lettings become protected tenancies by virtue of section 1 of the Act. Whether they are periodic or for a fixed term makes no difference.

Where the landlord is resident, and the furnished letting remains a Part VI contract under the Rent Act 1968, new section 5A (5) (b) (added to the Rent Act 1968 by paragraph 1 of Schedule 2, Part I, of the new Act) has the effect of making further fixed term contracts with the same tenant protected tenancies.

The desire to obviate a device for evading control is understandable. However, less desirable is the retrospective legislative effect of the way this has been done. Many absentee landlords have granted fixed term tenancies genuinely because of their personal circumstances in the belief they could regain possession of their property at the end of the term. Now they will not be able to do so, unless they can prove one of the Cases within Schedule 3 of the Rent Act 1968. There seems to be no good reason why these existing fixed term contracts should not have been exempted to prevent the personal hardships which are bound to arise leaving the new provisions to operate against future fixed term contracts. Examples have been given of purchases of future homes by civil servants posted abroad; members of the armed forces abroad; purchases for future redevelopment; a purchase for an aged relative pending a local authority compulsory purchase order for his home; all with fixed term lettings granted meanwhile. Unless the owners can show they actually lived in the house at some time or have actually retired the prospects of their recovering their property at the end of the fixed term are grim.

RENT ALLOWANCES

The Act further assimilates the law relating to furnished and unfurnished accommodation by restructuring the schemes for payment of rent allowances. The effect of the new provisions is to make the same rate of allowance payable whether the letting is furnished or unfurnished. Previously the allowance for furnished premises was increased by 25% over and above that which would have been payable if the accommodation were unfurnished. Also the rule that tenants of furnished accommodation under the age of 30 without dependent children or a pensioner or handicapped person living with them are ineligible for rent allowances is abolished. At the same time regulations are to be introduced to ensure that students do not receive an accommodation subsidy from public funds twice over once through their grants and once through the rent allowance.

EXTENSION OF THE ACT

The Act applies to England, Wales and Scotland but not to Northern Ireland.

ROYAL ASSENT: 31st July 1974—Commencement: 14th August 1974.

B.—COMMENTARY ON SECTIONS

SECTION 1.—EXTENSION OF PROTECTION TO FURNISHED TENANCIES

It is this section which removes the bar which hitherto prevented furnished tenancies from having the same protection afforded to unfurnished tenants by the Rent Act 1968 and the Rent (Scotland) Act 1971 (hereinafter referred to as the Rent Acts). The distinction between furnished and unfurnished tenancies had been already blurred by *Woodward v. Docherty* (*see* p. 2, *supra*).

The section provides that furnished tenancies, now brought into protection by the Rent Act 1974 (hereinafter referred to as this Act), shall be regulated tenancies; and that the provisions of the Rent Acts shall apply subject to the modifications contained in Schedule 1 to this Act.

Subsection (1) (*a*)—this provides that, on or after the commencement date (14th August 1974), a tenancy shall no longer be prevented from being a protected tenancy, for the purposes of the Rent Acts, only by reason of the fact that the rent includes payment for the use of furniture.

Such furnished tenancies must of course satisfy the Rent Acts requirements for protected tenancies namely they must be:—

    (i) of a dwellinghouse let as a separate dwelling, and

    (ii) of a rateable value within the limits laid down by section 6 of this Act, and

    (iii) by a landlord which is not an exempted body, *e.g.* a local authority, housing association, etc.

Certain tenancies excluded from protection continue to remain outside the Rent Acts namely those:—

    (*a*) let at a low rent or no rent;

    (*b*) *bona fide* let at a rent which includes payment for board or attendance;

    (*c*) let with land other than their own site;

    (*d*) agricultural holdings.

To this list are added three new exempted classes of tenancies (*see* section 2, *below*).

Additionally, Schedule 3 (Transitional Provisions) prevents existing furnished tenancies by resident landlords becoming protected tenancies and Schedule 2, Part I, all future tenancies granted by resident landlords whether furnished or unfurnished.

Subsection (1) (*b*)—this has the effect of ensuring that the furnished tenants brought into protection by this Act will be treated as protected tenants for the purpose of all existing legislation relating to the Rent Acts, *e.g.* the Housing Acts, Land Compensation Acts, Matrimonial Causes Act, etc.

In other words all the benefits of a protected tenancy are extended to furnished tenants affected by section 1.

Subsection (2)—this defines references to a protected furnished tenancy, a regulated furnished tenancy, and a statutory furnished tenancy as references to existing or future tenancies which are protected tenancies by virtue of this Act.

There are differentiations within this Act between tenancies previously protected and those which become protected as a result of this Act. For example in section 13 below, where a sub-tenant becomes the tenant of a superior landlord.

Subsection (3)—this ensures no furnished tenancy which is protected by this Act can become a controlled tenancy despite the provisions of section 7 or Schedule 2 of the Rent Act.

The effect is that it will be a regulated tenancy with the rent fixed by the Rent Officer. (NOTE: the jurisdiction of the Rent Tribunal over all these furnished tenancies is thereby taken away.)

Subsection (4)—this provides for the repeal of the words " use of furniture " in section 2 (1) (*b*) of the Rent Act which preclude furnished tenancies from being protected tenancies. This is consequential upon subsection (1) above.

The subsection also provides for modifications to various parts of the Rent Act as set out in the three parts of Schedule 1 of this Act (*infra*).

SECTION 2.—CERTAIN TENANCIES NOT TO BE PRO-TECTED

This section contains the three new kinds of tenancies which will not be eligible to full protection:—

- (*a*) lettings to students by educational institutions;
- (*b*) lettings for the purpose of a holiday;
- (*c*) lettings by resident landlords.

Provision is also made to apply the provisions of the Rent Acts where accommodation is shared with the landlord or other tenants subject to Schedule 2 of this Act.

Subsection (1)—this provides for the addition to the exempt tenancies listed in section 2 of the Rent Act the following further exemptions:—

- (i) A tenancy granted to a person who pursues or intends to pursue a course of study provided by a specified educational institution where the landlord is an educational institution whether corporate or incorporate.

Therefore with regard to students three differing sets of circumstances may arise:—

- (*a*) where the student is resident in college or a hall of residence or a building of which his university or any other educational establishment is his landlord. In such cases, the student cannot acquire permanent security of tenure and thus it is ensured that the accommodation is available for subsequent generations of students. Whether a student in such circumstances is a tenant or a licensee remains open to doubt as is the question whether a Rent Tribunal has jurisdiction.
- (*b*) where the student takes rooms or digs in a resident landlady's house. Here the general resident landlord exception applies.
- (*c*) where the student takes a flat or house without a resident landlord. Here full protection applies.

SECTION 2.—CERTAIN TENANCIES NOT TO BE PROTECTED

This last case has caused considerable anxiety to university authorities who have made representations to Members of Parliament that there are already indications that many land-lords will no longer let to students. Consequently, in the Lords an attempt was made to amend this Act so as to exclude from protection all persons pursuing specified courses of study. This amendment was removed by the Government in the Commons on the basis that exemption must be based on the nature of the accommodation not the attributes of the tenant.

In the Commons, an attempt was made by the opposition to ease the position by exempting all privately let accommodation as approved by the educational institution where the student is studying. The Minister announced that he would be introducing regulations that would permit the registration of student accommodation with educational institutions and thereby gain exemption. He admitted that this will require fresh legislation which could take two years before it became operative. A student accommodation crisis may well develop if the fears of the university authorities are realised.

(ii) A tenancy whose purpose is to confer the right to occupy for a holiday.

With the inclusion of furnished tenancies in the scope of protection it might be possible for holiday lettings, if not expressly excluded, to qualify for full protection. The wording follows section 70 (5) of the Rent Act which excluded holiday lettings from Part VI (Part VII in Scotland) of that Act.

The test as to what is "the purpose of the tenancy" does not necessarily rely upon the language used by the parties in their agreement. Reference must be made to the underlying circumstances. Any dispute may be referred to the Court under section 105 of the Rent Act 1968 (section 122 of the Rent (Scotland) Act 1971) which may look behind the words to determine the true purpose.

Subsection (2)—this provides by adding a subsection to section 2 of the Rent Act that "a specified educational institution" for the purpose of student exemption must be one of a

specified in regulations to be made by the Secretary
t is understood that the institutions will be those
higher or further education with local or central
government support either directly or through student grants
for the courses they provide.

It is to be noted that the landlord institution need not be
the same as the institution providing the course, for the
exemption to apply. This allows for the situation where a
college with spare accommodation may take in another's
students. It will not apply to residential accommodation let
by a college as an investment and not to provide for the student
body.

Subsection (3)—this provides for the resident landlord
exemption for *future* lettings. It does this by adding a new
section 5A after section 5 of the Rent Act 1968 which is that
which lists the exempt classes of landlords. The new section
is set out in detail in Schedule 2, Part I, of this Act.

This subsection also sets out a sub-paragraph to section 1
of the Rent Act 1968 (which defines a protected tenancy), the
effect of which is to exclude from protection a tenancy for
the whole of the period during which there is a resident
landlord.

[NOTE: the resident landlord exemption in respect of existing
furnished lettings is preserved by the transitional provisions
contained in Schedule 3, paragraph 1 (1).]

Subsection (4)—this relates to the provisions in the Rent
Acts which govern the security available to tenants sharing
accommodation either with their landlords or with other
tenants; and also the protection of those subletting part of
their own accommodation. Matters relating to the jurisdiction
of the County Courts and the local authority's power to provide
information are also covered.

This Act affects those provisions in varying degrees by way
of Schedule 2 (*see below*).

SECTION 3.—RECOVERY OF POSSESSION IN CERTAIN TENANCIES

The effect of this section is to provide a method of recovering possession in three specified circumstances.

A—where an owner wishes to recover a dwelling-house he acquired for his retirement.

B—where a holiday landlord has let holiday accommodation out-of-season.

C—where an educational institution lets student accommodation temporarily to a non-student rather than leave it empty.

The method used is to add relevant cases to Part II of the 3rd Schedule of the Rent Acts which is that which specifies where it is mandatory upon the Court to make a possession order notwithstanding that the dwelling-house is subject to a regulated tenancy.

Subsection (1)—this applies to England and Wales and adds three new cases to Part II, 3rd Schedule, of the Rent Act 1968.

The first case is *Case 10A*.

This requires the County Court to grant an order for possession where an owner wants back the house he acquired for his own retirement, subject to the following conditions:—

(a) the owner served upon the regulated tenant a notice either at the beginning of the tenancy, or, if the tenancy is in existence on the passing of this Act, within six months of the 31st July 1974. The notice must make it clear that the owner would require possession on his retirement, and

(b) since the 14th August 1974, the landlord has not let the property on a protected tenancy without service of such a notice, and

(c) the Court is satisfied that the owner has retired from regular employment and requires the property to live in it or that the owner has died and it is needed as a residence of a member of his family living with him at the time of his death.

There is a proviso giving the Court discretion to dispense with the service of the notices where it deems it just and equitable. This proviso will cover the circumstances where a landlord did not know of the need to serve a written notice or could not do so in time because he was abroad. It is open to doubt whether a Judge will exercise his discretion in the case of professional negligence by the landlord's solicitors or agents.

This case will not assist an owner to recover a retirement home which he requires before his retirement because of change in his personal circumstances. In such an event he must firstly try to rely on Case 10 which, however, will only be available to him if he occupied the dwelling as his own home before the letting; but the order will still be mandatory. If he did not so reside, then he may be able to rely upon Case 8 on the grounds he reasonably requires the dwelling as a residence for himself. Here the house will have to have been bought before 24th May 1974 and order for possession is discretionary. Also the Court will consider whether the landlord or tenant will suffer greater hardship.

These two Cases 10 and 8 are not as satisfactory from the owner's point of view as 10A because of prescribed dates contained in them.

The second case is *Case 10B*.

This requires the County Court to grant an order for possession of holiday accommodation which has been let out-of-season on a fixed term tenancy of not more than eight months.

The object is to ensure that holiday landlords are not forced out of business by protection given to their out-of-season tenants, or by being obliged to leave the accommodation empty and unproductive during the winter months.

The conditions for this case to apply are that:—

(a) the landlord gives notice that the property will be required for a holiday letting at the end of the fixed term. The notice must be given, as before, at the commencement of the tenancy or within 6 months of the passing of this Act;

(b) the premises were occupied at some time within the
twelve months previous to the commencement of the
tenancy or six months prior to the passing of this Act
under a right to occupy for a holiday.

In this case there does not appear to be any power given to
the Court to dispense with service of the notice. The intention
is presumably to ensure that the tenant is aware of the situation
from the inception.

The requirement that the dwelling-house was occupied
within the previous year on a holiday letting is to prevent abuse.
This method was chosen in preference to that requiring a
landlord to produce proof of future holiday lettings. The
reason is that Parliament felt it would be difficult to devise an
adequate test on which the Court could make a judgement
which would not be a disincentive to landlords to continue the
practice of out-of-season lettings.

The case however is not of much help to an owner who in
some years might wish to occupy the accommodation for his
own family holiday or let his own holiday home out-of-season.
The Minister took the view that second homes were not socially
desirable.

For the purposes of this case, a term of years certain is
defined as one which includes a tenancy which is liable to
determination by re-entry or by any other event other than by
landlord's notice.

The third case is *Case 10C*.

This requires the County Court to grant an order for
possession where a specified educational institution (*see*
section 2) has granted a term of years certain not exceeding
twelve months and requires possession at the expiration of the
term.

The conditions for this section to apply are that:—

(a) the institution gives notice that the accommodation
will be required at the end of the term. The notice
must be given at the commencement of the term or
within six months of the passing of the Act;

(*b*) the accommodation was occupied at some time within
the twelve months previous to the commencement of
the tenancy or six months prior to the passing of this
Act by a person pursuing a course of study provided
by a specified educational institution.

The object of this case is to enable universities and colleges
to receive rental income from their student accommodation in
between student lettings. It may happen that a research
student from abroad is delayed in taking up his course and
rather than leave the accommodation empty pending his arrival
the college may let without fear of creating a protected tenancy.
To prevent abuse in respect of pure investment lettings a
twelve month period is prescribed within which there must have
been a genuine prior student letting.

Subsection (2)—this provides that cases equivalent to 10A,
10B, and 10C above namely Cases 11A, 11B and 11C, shall
be added to Part II of Schedule 3 of the Rent (Scotland)
Act 1971.

These are provided as separate cases to cover the difference
in terminology under Scottish law. Otherwise their provisions
are identical.

Subsection (3)—this enables the Courts to dispense with
service of notices at the commencement of a tenancy in Case 10
(Case 11 in Scotland) of Part II of the 3rd Schedule of the Rent
Acts where this is just and equitable. These cases relate to
where an owner-occupier wants back possession from a regulated tenant so as to be able to live in his own home in which
he has previously lived. (*See* Case 10A *above*.)

SECTION 4.—ADVANCE APPLICATION FOR REGISTRA-
TION OF A NEW RENT

This section enables a landlord to apply on his sole application to a rent officer for a new rent to be registered in respect
of a dwelling-house before the normal registration period of
three years has expired so that the new rent may start to
operate immediately the three years are up.

Under section 44 (3) of the Rent Act 1968, a landlord alone may not apply for registration of a rent different from that on the register unless three years have expired since the last registered rent was confirmed or there has been a change in circumstances.

This section of this 1974 Act permits an application to be made by the landlord alone within three months from the end of the three years to take effect on the day after the expiration of the three years.

Subsection (1)—this provides for a new subsection (3A) to be added to section 44 of the Rent Act 1968 providing for an application by a landlord alone within the last three months of the three year registration period.

Subsection (2)—this provides for the addition of a new subsection (1A) to section 48 of the Rent Act 1968 so that the registration of the rent determined under subsection (1) above may take effect on the day after the expiration of the three years registration period relating to the previous rent.

Subsections (3) and (4)—these provide for new subsections (3A) and (1A) to sections 40 and 44 respectively of the Rent (Scotland) Act 1971 similar in effect to those added to sections 44 and 48 of the Rent Act 1968 as mentioned above.

SECTION 5.—TRANSITIONAL PROVISIONS AFFECTING FURNISHED LETTINGS WHICH BECOME FURNISHED TENANCIES

This section covers the situations in which existing furnished lettings, becoming protected tenancies as a result of this Act, are at the date of transmutation subject to requirements resulting from the previous application to them of Part VI (Part VII Scotland) of the Rent Act.

Subsection (1)—where a rent has been registered under Part VI of the Rent Act as the result of a reference to a Rent Tribunal that rent remains the maximum rent recoverable whilst it is let as a furnished letting.

This subsection has the effect of deeming the Part VI registration to be a Part IV registration (*i.e.* the regulated rent) because Part IV will govern the tenancy from the commencement of this Act. The Part VI rent therefore remains the maximum rent until replaced by an actual Part IV registration.

The effective date for the deemed Part IV registration is the commencement date of this Act, *viz.* 14th August 1974.

Subsection (2)—this provides that section 44 (3) of the Rent Act (section 40 (3) Scotland) shall not have the effect of precluding an application for a Part IV registration where there is a deemed registration under the preceding subsection.

The need for this subsection is that section 44 (3) (and section 40 (3) for Scotland), provides that where a rent has been registered under Part IV no fresh application by the landlord or tenant alone may be entertained within three years of the effective date unless there is a change in circumstances. It is felt that this is inappropriate where the registration under Part IV is deemed to have occurred especially as the Part VI registration may be years old.

Subsection (3)—this has the effect of enabling an application to be made for a certificate of fair rent notwithstanding that subsection (1) above deems a registration of a Part IV rent.

Section 45 of the Rent Act (section 41 Scotland) enables a landlord to apply to a rent officer for a certificate as to what the fair rent shall be of any intended letting. Under section 45 (1) (*b*) (section 41 (1) (*b*) Scotland), he may not do this if a fair rent has been registered within the last three years.

Under section 4 (3) of this Act a deemed rent is excluded from the effects of section 45 (1) (*b*) (section 41 (1) (*b*) Scotland).

It is to be noted that certificates of fair rents may now be obtained from rent officers where the landlord is a non-resident *i.e.* where they have become protected tenancies by this Act. This Act has made no provision for a certificate where the landlord is resident.

Subsection (4)—this provides for the situation where a furnished tenant is under a notice to quit at the time this Act converts his tenancy into a protected tenancy AND the operation of the notice is suspended by an application to a Rent Tribunal made under Part VI of the 1968 Rent Act.

In such circumstances, the temporary security of the Rent Tribunal application becomes permanent security as with any other protected tenant.

The subsection does not apply where the suspension of the notice to quit has expired before the 14th August 1974. Nor does it affect furnished tenancies which remain under Part VI of the 1968 Rent Act, *e.g.* where the landlord is resident in the building.

The subsection does not debar a landlord from applying to the Courts for possession in any case where he has grounds for doing so in respect of a protected tenant. Thus the subsection provides that the suspended notice shall take effect on the day following 14th August 1974.

SECTION 6.—FURNISHED LETTINGS—INCREASE IN RATEABLE VALUES

This section brings further furnished lettings, which do not become protected tenancies, within the ambit of Part VI of the Rent Act 1968 by raising the rateable value limits which apply to such lettings. It does not apply to protected tenancies which have already had their rateable value limits increased by the Counter-Inflation Act 1973. All rented accommodation therefore becomes subject to the same rateable value limits. The section will have the greatest practical effect in respect to furnished lettings where there is a resident landlord.

Under the Rent Act 1965, all rented accommodation, furnished and unfurnished, had the same rateable value limits, namely £400 in Greater London and £200 outside. Section 89 of the Housing Finance Act 1972 enabled these limits to be increased by Order following the 1973 rating revaluation. An order was made in respect of furnished accommodation raising the rateable value limits for these to £1,000 and £500 respectively. However, section 89 above was repealed in so far as it related to protected tenancies by the Counter-Inflation Act 1973 which raised the limits to £1,500 and £750 respectively for such tenancies as from 1st April 1973.

Broadly speaking, the old rateable value of £400 is equivalent to a new rateable value of £1,000 and one of £200 to a new one of £500. Therefore the effect of the increase of the limits is to bring a wider range of rented accommodation within rent control. The new rateable value of £1,500 for Greater London is roughly equivalent to the old £600 and the new £750 for outside to the old £300.

This section operates by adding a new subsection (1) to section 71 of the Rent Act 1968 and by substituting a new subsection (1A) for the old subsection (1) which is repealed.

New subsection (1) of section 71, Rent Act 1968—this relates to dwellings which appeared in the valuation list before 1st April 1973.

Lettings of such dwellings will be subject to Part VI of the Rent Act 1968 if they

> *either* (*a*) had on the 23rd March 1965, or the date on which they first appeared on the valuation list if later, a rateable value not exceeding £400 inside or £200 outside Greater London
>
> *or* (*b*) had on the 1st April 1973 a rateable value not exceeding £1,500 inside or £750 outside Greater London.

These alternatives exist to cover the possibility that a dwelling within the pre-1973 limits might fall outside the 1973 limits on revaluation and so prevent a tenant falling out of protection.

New Subsection (1A)—this relates to dwellings appearing in the valuation lists for the first time on or after 1st April 1973 and provides that Part VI shall apply to them if the rateable values do not exceed £1,500 inside and £750 outside London.

The section has no application to Scotland.

It appears from a sample survey made by Chestertons, Estate agents of London, that the new rateable value limits as they apply to furnished tenancies will bring into rent officer and rent tribunal control accommodation which commands rents of up to £90 per week. Since the object of this Act is to protect families in areas of housing stress from threat of eviction from their permanent homes, the need to extend the rateable value limits to this extent seems most questionable. However, the Government resisted amendments to reduce the values both in the Commons and the Lords.

SECTION 7.—FURNISHED LETTINGS: AMENDMENTS RELATING TO CONTROL AND REGISTRATION OF RENTS

This section brings closer the amalgamation of the systems for determining and registering the rents of protected and Part VI tenancies. It does this by amending the power of Rent Tribunals under Part VI.

Subsection (1)—this gives a general power to Rent Tribunals for the very first time to *increase* rents where a Part VI contract is referred to them. Previously under section 73 of the Rent Act 1968, a Rent Tribunal could only confirm or decrease a rent or dismiss a tenant's application.

This general power renders unnecessary the limited power of Rent Tribunals to increase rents in the restricted circumstances of:—

    (*a*) certain long-standing contracts under section 73 (3)

and (*b*) registered rents where there have been changes of circumstances under section 75 (2).

Both these are now repealed.

Subsection (2)—this provides that where a rent has been registered under Part VI of the Rent Act 1968, a Rent Tribunal need not entertain a reference to review the rent unless:—

    (*a*) it is on a joint application by both landlord or tenant

or   (*b*) more than three years have elapsed since the registration

or   (c) the reference is made on the grounds that there has
        been a change in condition of the dwelling, the furni-
        ture, the terms of the contract or any other circum-
        stances taken into account when the rent was last
        considered with the consequence that the rent is no
        longer reasonable.

This subsection replaces section 73 (5), Rent Act 1968, which
provided that a Rent Tribunal shall not be required to entertain
a reference other than by a local authority to review a registered
rent if they were satisfied that, having regard to the length of
time elapsing since a previous application by the same party,
that the reference is frivolous or vexatious.

The effect of the subsection is to allow a Rent Tribunal to
entertain a reference because changes in circumstances have
rendered the previous rent to be no longer reasonable.   This
replaces the previous requirement that the Rent Tribunal had
to have regard primarily to the time which had elapsed since
the previous reference.

It remains to be seen how Rent Tribunals and the Courts
will interpret " change of circumstances ", but the new provision appears to be wide enough to cover the effects of inflation
upon costs of maintenance, repairs and replacement of
furniture.

Another effect of the subsection is to *require* a Rent Tribunal
to entertain references after 3 years from the date of the
tribunal's previous consideration.

Subsection (3)—this requires the inclusion in the Register of
Rents under Part VI, where rates are borne by the landlord or
a superior landlord, a note to that effect.   This will not, however, affect the amount of the rent registered.

Subsection (4)—this makes drafting amendments to section
75 (1) of the Rent Act 1968 consequential upon the general
power given under subsection (1) above to Rent Tribunals to
increase rent.

Subsection (5)—this provides that, where the fact that rates
are borne by the landlord is noted on the register under subsection (3) above, the amount of rent for any rental period

may be increased by the amount of rates for that period ascertained in accordance with the 4th Schedule of the 1968 Rent Act.

The object is to enable the landlord to recover the increases in rates for any rental period in addition to the Registered Rent without contravening the provisions of section 76 (1) of the Rent Act 1968.

Section 76 (1) provides that a landlord cannot require or receive more than the registered rent in respect of a Part VI contract. Section 76 (3) makes contravention a criminal offence.

This subsection in effect amends section 76 by adding a new subsection (1A), dealing with the rates of inclusive rents as mentioned above.

Subsection (6)—this defines " rental period " for the purposes of the section.

SECTION 8.—FURNISHED LETTINGS: AMENDMENTS RELATING TO SECURITY OF TENURE

This section amends provisions in the Rent Act 1968 relating to the security of tenure which may be granted by Rent Tribunals in respect of Part VI contracts.

Subsection (1)—this enables a Rent Tribunal to give a security of tenure of up to six months even where it has granted a period of security of less than six months on a preceding application by the tenant.

This is achieved by deleting section 78 (1) (c) of the Rent Act 1968 which prevented a tenant from applying for an extension of a period of security of tenure where, on a previous application by that tenant, the Rent Tribunal had granted a period of security of less than six months under its powers contained in section 77 (1) (a) of the Rent Act.

Subsection (2)—this enables a Rent Tribunal to reduce security of tenure for a period of less than six months where the tenant or anyone residing with him so ill-treats the furniture provided by the landlord as to cause it to deteriorate.

This is achieved by adding a subsection (*d*) to section 80 (2) of the Rent Act 1968. Section 80 stipulates three cases in which the Rent Tribunal may direct a lesser period than six months for security namely breach of contract, acts of nuisance or annoyance or use of the premises for illegal or immoral purposes, and deterioration of the dwelling by act or neglect of the tenant or anyone residing with him.

The Government originally intended in this clause to extend the six months' periods of security to twelve months, but abandoned this under pressure.

SECTION 9.—SCOTLAND: FURNISHED LETTINGS: AMENDMENTS TO CONTROL AND REGISTRATION OF RENTS

This section is similar to section 7 which relates to England and Wales. It makes amendments to the Rent (Scotland) Act 1971 having the same effect as the section 7 amendments to the Rent Act 1968.

SECTION 10.—SCOTLAND: FURNISHED LETTINGS: AMENDMENTS RELATING TO SECURITY OF TENURE

This section makes similar amendments to the Rent (Scotland) Act 1971 as section 8 makes to the Rent Act 1968 for England and Wales.

SECTION 11.—RENT ALLOWANCES: ENGLAND AND WALES

This section is consequential upon the underlying principle of the Act that the distinction between furnished and unfurnished accommodation is abolished for most purposes. Hence, the clause seeks to assimilate the rules under the Housing Finance Act 1972 for the purpose of the payment of rent allowances whether to furnished or unfurnished tenants.

The principal changes made to produce a single system of rent allowances are:—

> (i) the abolition of the rule that the tenant of furnished accommodation must be over the age of 30 to qualify for a rent allowance;

    (ii) provision for the avoidance of an overlap of rent allowances and student grants as a result of (i);

    (iii) the abolition of the mark up of 25% on rent allowances for furnished accommodation.

Subsection (1)—this provides that the Secretary of State may make regulations obviating the requirement that a tenant of furnished accommodation under a Part VI letting must be a " qualified person " to be eligible for a rent allowance. The power to define a " qualified person " is contained in section 19 (12) added to the Housing Finance Act 1972 by the Furnished Lettings (Rent Allowances) Act 1973.

It is understood that the Secretary of State will appoint the 30th September 1974 as the date upon which it will no longer be necessary to be a " qualified person " to claim the rent allowance for furnished accommodation. This is to give time for necessary publicity and to enable local authorities to make the necessary administrative changes.

Under existing provisions " qualifying persons " are Part VI tenants who are pensioners, have a pensioner living with them, handicapped persons, those with a dependent child, or persons aged 30 or over. There are also residential qualifications for some of these categories varying from 3 to 6 months.

The result is that most Part VI contract holders below 30 years of age are not qualified persons and so are ineligible for a rent allowance.

The change in this situation has become necessary because those with non-resident landlords will become protected tenants and no longer within Part VI. It would be inequitable for them thereby to qualify automatically for rent allowances leaving those with resident landlords ineligible.

The abolition of the qualified person requirement for Part VI tenants will therefore both lift restrictions and simplify the rent allowance scheme.

Subsection (2)—this provides for the abolition of the provision under which the eligible rent may reflect a 25% mark up.

Rent allowances are based upon the occupational element of the rent, *i.e.* the rent net of any sums attributable to rates, services, or furniture.   Where no rent has been registered, the local authority is required to arrive at the eligible rent by estimating the fair rent.   In the case of furnished dwellings, this estimated fair rent could be increased by a quarter provided this does not exceed the rent actually paid.

The mark up is being removed again so as not to create a disparity in rent allowances between those tenants with a resident landlord and those without.

This change came into force immediately on the 14th August 1974 so that no new allowances for Part VI tenants can be calculated on the basis of the 25% mark up.

Subsections (3), (4) and (5)—these provide that Part VI tenants already in receipt of a rent allowance with the 25% mark up, *i.e.* as at 14th August 1974, may retain it at its present level until either:—

(*a*) existing provisions produce a higher eligible rent, *e.g.* as rents increase;

or (*b*) they cease to occupy the dwelling as their home on or after 14th August 1974;

or (*c*) the enhanced allowance is otherwise extinguished by change of circumstances;

or (*d*) the rent legally recoverable is less than the former eligible rent, *e.g.* by a registration under section 46 or section 74 of the Rent Act 1968;

or (*e*) a tenant either sub-lets part of his tenancy when he has not previously done so before 14th August 1974 or having done so becomes entitled to a higher rent from his sub-tenant.

Subsection (6)—this is a drafting amendment to clarify the meaning of existing rent in section 25 (1) of the Housing Finance Act as amended by the Furnished Lettings (Rent Allowances) Act 1973.

Subsection (7)—provides for the making of regulations for deductions from the occupational element of rent for tenants who are also students in receipt of awards or grants.

This is because it is not felt justifiable to make rent allowances available on the normal basis to students who are already in receipt of assistance from public funds towards their rents.

The deduction will apply during term time in the case of university students and the regulations will specify the amounts and periods of the deductions and where necessary different periods for different kinds of awards or grants.

Subsections (8) and (9)—these widen the definition of " tenant " in section 26 (1) of the Housing Finance Act 1972 to include persons who are local authority tenants in furnished accommodation but treated as private tenants by virtue of the Furnished Lettings (Rent Allowances) Act 1973. The widened definition is applied to subsections (1) to (5) above, so that, for example, such tenants would, if otherwise eligible, be entitled to the benefit of the transitional provisions concerning the 25% mark up.

SECTION 12.—RENT ALLOWANCES: SCOTLAND

This section applies similar modifications to the rules relating to Rent Allowances in Scotland as section 11 applies to England and Wales.

SECTION 13.—EFFECT ON FURNISHED SUB-TENANCY OF DETERMINATION OF SUPERIOR UNFURNISHED TENANCY

This section modifies, as regards protected and furnished tenancies, the effects of section 18 of the Rent Act 1968 and of section 17 of the Rent (Scotland) Act 1971. These sections provide that where a tenant has lawfully granted a sub-tenancy which is a protected or statutory tenancy under the Act, and the tenancy of this intermediate tenant/landlord comes to an end, the sub-tenant becomes the tenant of the superior landlord on the same terms as those he held from the tenant/landlord whose intermediate interest has disappeared.

These provisions could cause difficulty where the intermediate tenant/landlord had held on an unfurnished basis and then provided furniture or services for his sub-tenant.

Therefore, the section provides that, in such circumstances, the superior landlord shall not be obliged to provide the former sub-tenant with the furniture or services previously supplied by the intermediate tenant/landlord. He may, of course, accept the obligation if he so wishes.

Services are included because they are frequently undertaken by landlords in respect of furnished lettings but rarely where the tenancy is unfurnished.

Subsection (1)—this provides that where the relevant conditions are fulfilled, sections 18 and 17 (*supra*) shall not have the effect of imposing on the superior landlord any terms as to the provision of furniture or services.

Subsection (2)—this sets out the relevant conditions which are:—

(*a*) the intermediate tenancy was not a protected or statutory furnished tenancy. The reason is that if the superior landlord had provided the furniture there is no point in his not continuing to do so;

(*b*) the sub-tenancy must be a protected or statutory furnished tenancy, *i.e.* as a result of the operation of this Act;

(*c*) the superior landlord must serve a notice within six weeks of the ending of the intermediate tenancy that he does not wish to undertake the obligation to provide furniture or services.

Thus the obligation to provide furniture and services will arise unless expressly repudiated within six weeks.

Nothing is said in the section as to what will be the position if the sub-tenant does not wish to give up the furniture of his former immediate landlord and the superior landlord declines to undertake the obligation to provide any. Presumably the intermediate landlord must rely upon an action in detinue against his former sub-tenant to recover his furniture.

No doubt in the majority of cases the intermediate landlord will come to an arrangement to sell the furniture either to the

superior landlord or the sub-tenant. If the sub-tenant purchases the furniture or delivers it up to his former landlord, no
doubt he will be able to apply to the rent officer for a variation
in the rent under section 24, Rent Act 1968.

SECTION 14.—POWER OF COURT IN ACTION FOR POSSESSION TO REDUCE PERIOD OF NOTICE TO QUIT

This section gives the County Court in England and Wales
and the Sheriff's Court in Scotland power to entertain actions
for possession in specific circumstances and to make an order
notwithstanding that the operation of a notice to quit has been
suspended and a period of security of tenure granted by a
reference to a Rent Tribunal.

It has been a longstanding grievance of landlords of furnished accommodation that it has been possible for bad tenants
to delay possession actions by using the Rent Tribunals to
obtain extended periods of security of tenure. An action for
possession would not lie until the periods of security, which
the Rent Tribunals were prepared to give, had been exhausted.
The result could be that the landlord faced considerable loss
of income, damage to his property, or had to endure anti-social
behaviour before obtaining his remedy at law.

The section now gives the landlord recourse directly to the
Courts in such circumstances.

In practice, this section will only be invoked by resident
landlords since with protected tenancies there is no Rent
Tribunal jurisdiction.

Subsection (1)—this adds a new section 80A to the Rent Act
1968. This new section provides that in any case where:—

(a) any notice to quit has been served in respect of a Part
VI contract, and

(b) the period of the notice to quit is for the time being
extended by security of tenure granted following a
reference to a Rent Tribunal under sections 77 or 78
of the Rent Act 1968, and

(*c*) at any time during the period of the security of tenure the landlord institutes proceedings for possession in the County Court, and

(*d*) the County Court is satisfied that

    (i) the tenant has not complied with the terms of the contract, or

    (ii) the tenant or anyone residing or lodging with him causes nuisance or annoyance to adjoining owners or has been convicted of using the premises for illegal or immoral purposes, or

    (iii) the condition of the premises has deteriorated due to an act or neglect by the tenant or anyone residing or lodging with him, or

    (iv) the condition of the furniture has deteriorated due to ill-treatment by the tenant or anyone residing or lodging with him

then the Court may direct that the security of tenure shall be reduced to a date which the Court shall determine; in other words, that possession shall be delivered up by the tenant.

Subsection (2)—this enables the Lord Chancellor to make rules as to the procedure of the Court to deal with applications for possession under the foregoing subsection (1).

It is to be presumed that the rules will provide for an expedited procedure to deal with the situation of a bad tenant envisaged by this section.

Subsection (3)—this adds a new section 95A to the Rent (Scotland) Act 1971 similar in effect to 80A above.

SECTION 15.—INTERPRETATION

This section sets out in subsection (1) the definitions of terms used in the Act.

Subsection (2) provides additionally that the interpretations used in the Rent Acts shall apply also to this Act.

Subsection (3) ensures that references in this Act to existing legislation shall be taken as references to that legislation as amended by any other legislation including this Act.

Subsection (1)—The definitions are:—

" Commencement Date ": the date on which the Act became law which by virtue of section 17 (5) below was 2 weeks after Royal Assent, namely the 14th August 1974.

" Dwelling ": in relation to a furnished letting this means a house or part of a house. This is here because no definition appears in Part VII of the Rent (Scotland) Act 1971 although the same definition is found in section 84 (1), Rent Act 1968.

" Furnished Letting ": a Part VI Contract (Part VII in Scotland) as defined by the Rent Acts.

" Protected Furnished tenancy, etc.": *see* section 1 (2) above.

" The Rent Act ": The Rent Act 1968 for England and Wales or the Rent (Scotland) Act 1971 for Scotland.

" Services ": as defined by the Rent Act, *i.e.* attendance, provision of heating or lighting, the supply of hot water and any other facilities provided other than access, cold water supply or sanitary accommodation.

Subsections (2) and (3)—*see* notes above.

SECTION 16.—TRANSITIONAL PROVISIONS AND REPEALS

Subsection (1)—provides that the transitional provisions set out in the 3rd Schedule to this Act shall have effect notwithstanding anything in the preceding provisions of this Act.

Subsection (2)—provides that the Repeals listed in the 4th Schedule to this Act shall take effect.

SECTION 17.—SHORT TITLE, ETC.

Subsection (1)—the Act shall be known as the Rent Act 1974.

Subsection (2)—this Act and the Rent Act 1968 shall be known as the Rent Acts 1968 and 1974.

Subsection (3)—this Act and the Rent (Scotland) Acts 1971 and 1972 shall be known as the Rent (Scotland) Acts 1971 to 1974.

Subsection (4)—the Furnished Houses (Rent Control) Act 1946 never applied to the Scilly Isles and hence Part VI does not apply.   This preserves the position.

Subsection (5)—this Act comes into operation two weeks after (14 August 1974) the date on which it was passed (31 July 1974).

Subsection (6)—this provides for the application of the appropriate parts of this Act to England and Wales and to Scotland.

Subsection (7)—this provides this Act shall not apply to Northern Ireland.

SCHEDULE 1.

CONSEQUENTIAL AMENDMENTS OF RENT ACT

PART I:

AMENDMENTS OF SCHEDULE 3 TO RENT ACT

The 3rd Schedule of the Rent Act 1968 lists in Part I the cases where a Court may make a possession order in respect of a protected or statutory tenancy and in Part II the cases where the Court must make an Order.

The 3rd Schedule is amended in this part of Schedule 1 of this Act.

A new ground for possession is introduced where a tenant ill-treats the furniture and modifications are made to the existing ground where a tenant overcharges his sub-tenant.

Other cases are amended as to dates so as to encompass the addition by this Act of furnished tenancies to protected tenancies.

" Suitable alternative accommodation " is also redefined.

Paragraph 1—this adds a new Case 3A to those in Part I of Schedule 3 of the Rent Act where the Court may make an order for possession.

This case applies where the protected furnished tenant, or anyone living or lodging with him or any sub-tenant of his so ill-treats the furniture as to cause its deterioration and if the ill-treatment was not carried out by the tenant himself he has not taken all reasonable steps to remove the lodger or sub-tenant.

Paragraph 2—this provides that the 14th August 1974 shall be substituted for 8th December 1965 in Case 5 in respect of tenancies brought into protection by this Act. Case 5 enables the Court to make an order for possession where a tenant has assigned or sublet without landlord's consent, after the specified date.

Paragraph 3—this provides that the 24th May 1974 (date of publication of the Bill) shall be substituted for 23rd March 1965 in Case 8 where it applies to a protected furnished tenancy. This case applies where the landlord requires the house for himself or a member of his family but not where he bought the house after the given date.

The alteration in the date preserves the situation of existing owners but not those who bought after publication of the Bill.

Paragraph 4—this amends the wording of Case 9 where possession may be obtained if a tenant overcharges his sub-tenant. A sub-paragraph is added to Case 9 to the effect that the ground shall apply if the tenant is charging more for a part of his tenancy sublet on a Part VI contract than the maximum recoverable under Part VI.

Previously Case 9 did not apply to sublettings on Part VI contracts.

Paragraph 5—this provides in respect of furnished regulated tenancies, that in Case 10 (Case 11 in Scotland) the date 14th August 1974 shall be substituted for 8th December 1965. These cases relate to the owner-occupier recovering his own home. He cannot do so if let on a protected tenancy after the 14th August 1974 unless a required notice was served on the relevant date (*see* paragraph 6, below).

It also provides that the notice requirements of the cases are complied with if the notice was given before the commencement date under section 79 (section 94 Scotland) of the Rent Act, in the case of existing tenancies, *i.e.*, by a temporarily absent landlord in respect of his furnished home.

Paragraph 6—defines " relevant date " in respect of the various notices which have to be served by owner-occupiers, landlords of holiday out-of-season lettings, owners of retirement homes in respect of furnished regulated lettings.

The relevant date is either the date of the commencement of the tenancy or if the tenancy is in existence at the commencement of the Act, namely 14th August 1974, then within six months of the 14th August 1974.

Paragraph 7—this adds to the definition of " suitable alternative accommodation " in respect of furnished tenancies. If in such tenancies the landlord wishes to satisfy the Court that he may have an order for possession because there is suitable alternative accommodation available, he must show that the furniture provided in the alternative accommodation is similar to that already provided in the existing tenancy or reasonably suited to the tenant and his family's needs.

The provision is to protect the tenant who requires the continued use of furniture provided by his landlord.

PART II:

AMENDMENTS OF PARTS IV, VIII AND IX
RENT ACT 1968

This Part of Schedule 1 details those modifications to the Rent Act 1968 referred to in section 1 (4) of this Act.

These amendments are minor but technically necessary; consequential upon the extension of protection to furnished tenancies. Thus the fair rent formula is altered to take account of furniture, as are the provisions as to applications for a certificate of fair rent. The jurisdiction of the County Courts is extended together with the powers of local authorities to provide information. Furnished sublettings of unfurnished tenancies and mortgage provisions also give rise to appropriate modifications of the 1968 Act.

Paragraph 8—this provides that in addition to a change in the condition of the dwelling a change in the quantity, quality or condition of the furniture shall be a ground to reconsider a registered rent within the 3 years' period since last registration.

Paragraph 9—provides for the modification of section 46 of the Rent Act (determination of fair rent) so that the rent officer shall have regard to the quantity, quality and condition of any furniture provided under a tenancy when he determines a fair rent of a regulated tenancy.

It also provides he shall disregard any deterioration or improvement in the condition of the furniture attributable to the tenant.

Paragraph 10—this provides that sections 93 to 95 of the Rent Act 1968 which relate to mortgages of dwelling houses subject to regulated tenancies shall only apply to mortgages subsisting when the Act came into operation. The provisions on mortgages allow the Courts to mitigate hardship to mortgagors.

Paragraph 11—this provides for the deletion of the words "use of furniture" from section 103 (1) (*b*) of the Rent Act 1968 which provides that protection as against a superior landlord shall not be lost where the intermediate tenant/landlord sublets part of his premises on an unprotected tenancy. This amendment is necessary because of the removal of the words "use of furniture" from section 2 (1) (*b*) of the 1968 Act (*see* section 1 (4) (*a*) of this Act). Formerly these words excluded furnished tenancies from being protected.

Paragraph 12—this enables the County Courts to determine whether any tenancy is a protected, regulated or statutory furnished tenancy within the meanings created by this Act. A sub-section to this effect is added to section 105 of the Rent Act 1968 which prescribes the County Court jurisdiction.

Paragraph 13—this adds this Act to section 106 of the Rent Act 1968 so that the Lord Chancellor may have power to make rules of procedure of the Court to give effect to this Act.

Paragraph 14—this extends a local authority's power under section 107 of the Rent Act 1968 to publish information as to rights and duties conferred by this Act.

Paragraph 15—this amends Schedule 6, paragraph 10, of the Rent Act 1968 so that a rent officer may ascertain whether the particulars of furniture contained in an application for a certificate of fair rent accord with the quality, quantity and condition of the furniture actually provided. If he is satisfied he may register the rent.

Paragraph 16—this amends Schedule 7, paragraph 1, of the Rent Act 1968 which prescribes the form and contents of an application for a certificate of fair rent. The amendment requires the application to contain particulars of any furniture to be provided for use under a regulated tenancy.

PART III:

AMENDMENTS PART IV, IX AND X OF RENT (SCOTLAND) ACT 1971

This Part of Schedule 1 details those modifications to the Rent (Scotland) Act 1971 referred to in section 1 (4) of this Act.

They are all similar to the modifications made to the Rent Act 1968 by Part II of this Schedule and are comparable paragraph by paragraph.

SCHEDULE 2.

TENANCIES GRANTED BY RESIDENT LANDLORDS

PART I:

NO PROTECTION WHERE A RESIDENT LANDLORD

This establishes the second new principle underlying this Act; namely that, for the future, a tenant's protection shall be determined by whether or not his landlord lives within the same building. It replaces and, indeed, cuts across the former distinction which determined full protection; namely, as between furnished and unfurnished accommodation. The abolition of this former distinction is, of course, the first principle underlying this Act.

Part I of Schedule 2, therefore, lays down the criteria to be applied in determining whether or not protection will exist under the new principle relating to non-resident and resident landlords. This is done by adding a new section to the Rent Act 1968 and to the Rent (Scotland) Act 1971. The new section also spells out in detail who is a resident landlord and preserves his position where in certain circumstances he cannot be in residence.

Paragraph 1—this adds a new section 5A to the Rent Act 1968 the effect of which is to declare that a tenancy shall not be protected where the landlord's interest belongs to a resident landlord. It applies equally to furnished and unfurnished accommodation.

The conditions under which **new section 5A** will apply are:—

(1) the tenancy must be created on or after the 14th August 1974; and

(2) the tenancy must be of part of a building which was not originally constructed as a "purpose-built block of flats". [Therefore a landlord cannot live in one flat in a block of flats and claim that all the tenants in the block are not protected. However, if the building was originally built as a house, or even for commercial purposes, and is subsequently converted into flats or maisonettes, the landlord can do so. The object of this latter point is not to deter house-owners from converting the parts of their homes, which they do not need, into self-contained units which they can let. To propose otherwise would be to undermine the whole policy of successive Governments behind improvement grants which is to encourage such modernisation and conversion]; and

(3) the tenancy is granted by a landlord who is actually resident in the building of which the premises let form part. [The landlord must be in residence when he creates the tenancy]; and

(4) the landlord, or a successor in title, so remains in residence throughout the subsistence of the tenancy subject to certain permissible void periods mentioned below. [The object of this condition is to avoid a situation where a landlord may move into a building to grant tenancies and then moves out.]

Subsection (2) *of new section 5A* goes on to outline the periods of time during which a landlord may not be resident in the building without incurring the consequence of the tenancies within it becoming protected. These void periods to be disregarded are:—

(a) any period not exceeding 14 days during which there is a transfer of the landlord's legal or equitable interest in the building from one person to another. [This is an absolute period and begins with the date on which the transfer of the interest takes place and gives the new owner 14 days' grace in which to move in. The period is short because it is envisaged to cover in the main sales of property when it is usual for the purchaser to move into occupation and the vendor to move out on the day of actual completion of the conveyance on sale.]

(b) any period not exceeding 6 months provided that within the 14 days' grace given in (a) above, the new owner notifies the tenant in writing that it is his intention to move into and live in the building. [This is intended to cover situations where a vendor remains in occupation after completion date or the new owner does not move in because he wants to carry out repairs and decorations to his new home. It will be necessary for solicitors acting for purchasers of houses without full vacant possession to make it a standard practice to serve on completion a notice upon the tenants declaring their client's intention to take up residence within the 6 months.]

(c) any period not exceeding twelve months beginning with the date the landlord's interest becomes vested in personal representatives, the Probate Judge, or in trustees. [This is intended to cover the situation where a landlord in residence dies and his interest passes with his estate to personal representatives or to trustees if his interest was held subject to a trust or settlement. The twelve months are intended to cover the normal " executors' year ". However, a word of caution must be given. The twelve months does not begin with the date of the Probate of the will or the grant of Letters of Administration or any document by which the personal representatives seek to vest the property in themselves. Where there is a will, the property vests in the executors on the date of death and where there is an intestacy in the Probate Judge until the grant of representation is taken out. So the twelve months run from the date of death.]

Subsection (3) *of new section 5A*, deals with the situation where the landlord's legal title to the building is vested in trustees under a trust for sale and the actual residence is by the beneficiaries under the trust, who may or may not be the same persons as the trustees, but who nevertheless are not resident with a landlord's interest vested in them.

The subsection saves this situation in part by declaring that the resident landlord condition in 5A (1) (*c*) is satisfied if the residence is by the persons for whom the proceeds of sale of the trust are held.

The subsection also applies in the same way to a beneficiary in possession under a trust or settlement which is not a trust for sale.

Where a beneficiary under a trust is in residence no void period arises to be disregarded under subsection (2). BUT owing to an oversight by the Government provision is not made in subsection 5A (1) (*b*) for the granting of a tenancy by trustees for sale. Hence subsection (3) in trusts for sale has a limited value.

Practitioners will have to beware of a particularly nasty trap that has been laid for them by the way section 5A has been drafted. This is best explained by an example.

If a testator leaves his house by way of trust for sale for the benefit of his children on attaining majority with a right to his widow to occupy for as long as she wishes, the widow must not be permitted to sublet any part of the house *unless* she is also one of the trustees. This is because she will not be a person owning the interest of the landlord in occupation at the time the tenancy is granted within the meaning of 5A (1) (*b*). NOR must the trustees themselves grant the tenancy as they will not be in occupation. A solicitor executor will do so at his professional peril.

5A (3) is worded so as to save the situation for the trustees for sale only in so far as 5A (1) (*c*) is concerned, *i.e.* during any period *after* the tenancy is granted. It can therefore only operate where the testator himself originally created the tenancy.

The situation is, however, quite different where the will creates a strict settlement under the Settled Law Act 1925. Then the widow will be a tenant for life with all the powers of an estate owner and the legal estate vested in her.

In drafting wills therefore it may be necessary to abandon the modern practice of creating trusts for sale and reverting to strict settlements until such time as Parliament adds to 5A (3) a stipulation that " the condition in paragraph (*b*) of that sub-section shall also be deemed to be fulfilled ".

Subsection (4) *of new section* 5A provides that no Order for Possession may be obtained against a tenant during any period when there is no landlord in residence even though such a period is one which may be disregarded under subsection (2) above so as not to bring the tenancy into protection. This provision, however, does not preclude an Order which can be obtained against a regulated tenant, *i.e.* within any of the Cases of Schedule 3 of the Rent Act 1968. What it does is to preclude an Order which can only be obtained against a non-protected tenant, *e.g.* on the expiration of a notice to quit terminating the contractual tenancy.

The effect of this subsection, therefore, is to create a moratorium for the tenant as well as the landlord during the periods of landlord non-residence which otherwise may be disregarded under subsection (2).

Subsection (5) *of new section* 5A provides that the resident landlord exemption shall not apply in the two following cases:—

> (*a*) where the tenancy in question is granted to a person who was previously a protected tenant of a dwelling-house in the same building. This prevents a landlord depriving a tenant of protection by granting him a new tenancy either of the original accommodation or of

some other premises in the same building. Apart
from the provision it would be possible for a landlord
to move into a building which he did not previously
live in and by persuading his tenants to enter into new
agreements deprive them of security.

(b) where the tenancy in question is a fixed term contract
following upon a non-protected tenancy agreement
with the same tenant for a dwelling in any part of the
same building. The purpose of this provision is to
stop a landlord using a series of fixed term contracts as
a means of preventing his tenant applying to the Rent
Tribunal for security of tenure. [This provision
creates a curious situation. If a resident landlord
grants a fixed term letting to a *new* tenant, he will be
able to obtain possession at the end of the term without the Rent Tribunal granting any security of tenure,
because there is no notice to quit to be suspended.
However, if the landlord then allows the tenant to stay
on a periodic (*e.g.* weekly or monthly) tenancy he will
of course have to serve a notice to quit when he
requires possession which will enable the Rent Tribunal
to give security. But, if the landlord instead grants
the same tenant a further fixed term tenancy, that
tenancy becomes *fully protected*! A very dangerous
trap for the unwary owner and an incentive to the
worldly-wise to grant only first fixed term tenancies
and then be rid of the tenants at the end of each.
Hardly a desirable situation from the point of view of
either landlords or tenants.]

Subsection (6) *of new section* 5*A* defines a " purpose-built
block of flats ". It is a building which when it was originally
constructed contained and still contains two or more flats that
is to say dwellings within the same building separated from one
another horizontally. The minimal requirement of two flats
will serve to catch the many twin " maisonette " houses built
in the 1930's and between 1900 and 1914 for the owner-occupier
also requiring an income, but not the large Victorian family
house subsequently divided up into a number of separate living
units.

Subsection (7) *of new section* 5A seeks to define " occupation as a residence ". It does this by stating that the same conditions of residence are fulfilled as are required to be fulfilled by a statutory tenant under section 3 (2) of the Rent Act 1968. However, section 3 (2) construes " occupation of a dwelling-house as a residence " as " requiring the fulfilment of the same . . . qualifications as had to be fulfilled . . . to entitle a tenant within the meaning of the Increase of Rent and Mortgage Interest (Restrictions) Act 1920 to retain possession . . . ". The situation is not helped by the fact that the repealed 1920 Act does not itself define what these residential qualifications might be. One is therefore thrown upon the interpretation of that Act in the case of *Skinner v. Geary* [1931] 2 K.B. 546, and a large number of other cases referred by Megarry (10th Edition), pages 184-195.

Thus not only are we to construe landlord's residence by reference to what constitutes tenant's residence but are then lead through a maze of legislative definition and find " home " in case law. An example, which must rank high in the prize list for legislation by reference.

Paragraph 2—this incorporates a new section 5A in the Rent (Scotland) Act 1971, similar in intent to the new section 5A applying to England and Wales discussed in detail under paragraph 1 above. Modifications exist to make the provisions appropriate to Scottish law particularly with regard to succession, trusts and conveyancing of property.

PART II:

AMENDMENTS TO PART II, RENT ACT 1968

This part of the Schedule primarily introduces a new section 102A to the Rent Act 1968 which has the effect of applying Part VI of that Act to tenancies precluded from being protected tenancies by virtue of section 5A (inserted in the 1968 Act by Part I of this Schedule).

Paragraph 3—this is a drafting amendment to section 101 of the 1968 Act. It is necessary to ensure that tenancies in which

accommodation is shared with the landlord (as defined by
section 101) are brought within the terms of section 5A so that
they may also be treated as Part VI contracts by virtue of
paragraph 4 below.

Paragraph 4—this adds a new section 102A to the Rent Act
1968 so that all tenancies which are outside protection (because
of a resident landlord) become Part VI contracts and thereby
subject to Rent Tribunals whether furnished or unfurnished.

Subsection (1) *of new section* 102A—this declares that for so
long as a tenancy is precluded by new section 5A (*see* Part I
of this Schedule) from being a protected tenancy it shall be
treated as a contract within Part VI of the Rent Act 1968
whether or not furniture or services are provided.

Subsection (2) *of new section* 102A—this provides that where
5A ceases to apply to a tenancy and thereby it becomes protected, a rent registered under Part VI shall be deemed to be a
rent registered under Part IV from the date the protection
starts.

Subsection (3) *of new section* 102A—this provides that section
44 (3) of the Rent Act 1968 (which prohibits an application
for reregistration of rent within 3 years of the last registration
except for change of circumstances) shall not apply to a deemed
Part IV registration arising under subsection (2) above. (This
is similar to section 4 (2) of this Act.)

Subsection (4) *of new section* 102A—this provides that a rent
" deemed " to be registered under subsection (2) above shall
not be considered to be registered for the purposes of section
45 of the Rent Act 1968. This means that a rent registered
under Part VI will not prevent an application for a Certificate
of Fair Rent on the tenancy becoming protected by reason of
less than 3 years having elapsed since the rent was " deemed "
to be registered under Part IV. (This is similar to section 5 (3)
of this Act.)

Subsection (5) *of new section* 102A—this provides that where
a rent inclusive of rates is registered under a Part VI contract
by virtue of section 74 (2A) of the Rent Act 1968 (*see* section
7 (3) of this Act) and consequently a note made on the register

that the rates are borne by the landlord, then, when such a rent
is deemed to be registered under subsection (2) above, the Part
IV registration must operate and be noted similarly.

Subsection (6) *of new section* 102A—this provides that where
a tenancy, formerly exempt by section 5A, falls into protection,
then any notice to quit (served before protection befell) which
has not yet expired (including extensions given by a Rent
Tribunal) shall take effect on the day following the date the
tenancy becomes protected. This has the effect of making it
a statutory tenancy. (This provision is similar to section 5 (4)
of this Act.)

PART III:

AMENDMENT TO PART X, RENT (SCOTLAND) ACT 1971

Paragraphs 5 and 6.—These apply to the Rent (Scotland)
Act 1971 provisions similar to those applied by Part II to the
Rent Act 1968. A new section 119A is added applying Part
VII to tenancies falling within the new section 5A together with
the consequential modifications required by Scottish law.

SCHEDULE 3.

TRANSITIONAL PROVISIONS

This Schedule provides that existing furnished lettings by
landlords resident on the 14th August 1974 remain subject to
Part VI (or in Scotland Part VII) of the Rent Act for so long
as the landlord remains a resident landlord. It also makes
provision for those cases where a furnished tenancy has come
to an end before the 14th August 1974 but the tenant is still in
possession.

The Schedule therefore completes the overall Scheme of this
Act.

We have seen that section 1 of this Act has the effect of
bringing furnished tenancies into protection. This Schedule
precludes those furnished tenancies in existence where there is

a resident landlord from going into protection. The Second Schedule has already exempted all tenancies granted on or after the Act by a resident landlord from going into protection.

Therefore in protection are all furnished and unfurnished lettings by a non-resident landlord and all unfurnished lettings granted by a resident landlord before the Act. Out of protection are all furnished lettings with a resident landlord and all unfurnished lettings granted by a resident landlord after this Act.

Paragraph 1—this defines the criteria for establishing what furnished lettings in existence at the commencement of this Act shall not become protected furnished lettings by virtue of this Act.

Sub-paragraph (1)—states that where

(a) before the 14th August 1974 a tenancy was a furnished letting, and

(b) it is in respect of part of a building which is not a purpose-built block of flats, and

(c) on the 14th August 1974 the interest of the landlord belonged to a person occupying another part of the building as his residence or to trustees holding for a beneficiary in such occupation

then the tenancy shall be treated as granted on the 14th August 1974 under new section 5A of the Rent Act 1968 (*see* Schedule 2, Part I, above).

The effect of this is to exempt an existing furnished tenancy fulfilling the above conditions from becoming a protected tenancy.

Sub-paragraph (2)—omits certain provisions contained in new section 5A which are not appropriate to an existing furnished tenancy. These are those contained in subsection (5) of 5A; namely, exclusion from exemption where a new fixed term tenancy is granted or a new tenancy following upon a protected tenancy.

The sub-paragraph also incorporates the whole of this paragraph into the provisions of new section 102A (*see* Schedule 2,

Part II) which deals with the situation where an exempted furnished tenancy becomes a protected tenancy, *i.e.* where the landlord ceases to be a resident landlord.

Sub-paragraph (3)—this preserves the situation where all the conditions of sub-paragraph (1) apply, but the resident landlord had died before 14th August 1974 or created a settlement affecting the premises before that date with the consequence that there is temporarily no landlord in residence.

Sub-paragraph (4)—provides that the protection given to the landlord's interest by the preceding sub-paragraph shall run for 12 months from 14th August 1974.

After the expiration of that period if the affairs of the deceased's estate or of the settlement have not been put in order and no landlord is in residence once again, the tenancy will become protected.

Paragraph 1—this paragraph has a similar effect in Scotland as paragraph 1 has in England and Wales.

Paragraph 3—this makes provision for those furnished tenancies which would have been protected had they not terminated before the commencement of the Act and a tenant remains in possession. The intent is to put the tenants in the same position as if their tenancies had become protected (sub-paragraph (1)).

Sub-paragraph (2)—this applies to a furnished tenancy which has come to an end but no Court Order for Possession has yet been made. The sub-paragraph prohibits the making of the order unless it is one which could have been made against a protected tenant, *i.e.* under Schedule 3 of the Rent Act 1968.

Sub-paragraph (3)—this goes one stage further and applies where an Order for Possession has been made by the Court before the commencement of the Act, but has not been executed yet. In such a case, the tenant may apply back to the Court for rescission or variation of the order. The Court on such an application may rescind or vary the order if of the opinion that it would not have been made if the tenancy had been protected when it came to an end.

Sub-paragraph (4)—provides that a tenant remaining in possession after his tenancy has come to an end without an order for possession against him or after rescission of such an order shall be deemed to be a statutory tenant under a regulated tenancy. The statutory tenancy is further deemed to commence as on the termination of a protected tenancy and his tenancy which came to an end before the commencement of the Act shall be treated as—

(*a*) the original contract for the purpose of implying the terms and conditions of the statutory tenancy under section 12 of the Rent Act 1968;

(*b*) the previous contractual tenancy for the purposes of any proceedings under Case 8 of Schedule 3 (landlord requiring possession for himself or his family).

This is subject to any variations in the contractual terms made by the Court under sub-paragraphs (6) and (7) below.

Sub-paragraph (5)—this provides that where a rent has been registered under the Rent Act 1968 before the 14th August 1974 in respect of a tenancy which becomes a statutory tenancy by virtue of sub-paragraph (4) above, that rent shall be deemed to be registered under Part IV as at the 14th August 1974.

Sub-paragraph (6)—this gives the County Court in England and Wales full discretion to vary all or any of the terms of the statutory tenancy imposed by sub-paragraph (4) above.

Sub-paragraph (7)—this gives the Sheriff's Court in Scotland identical powers.

Sub-paragraph (8)—if the person who is in occupation at the 14th August 1974 is the person who would have been the first successor (that is, the appropriate co-resident relative at the date of the statutory tenant's death) if the previous tenancy had been protected before it came to an end, then under this sub-paragraph that person shall have the right to apply to the Court under sub-paragraph (3) and the right under sub-paragraph (4) to remain in occupation as statutory tenant. He will be the first successor under the statutory tenancy.

Paragraphs 4 and 5—these two paragraphs contain transitional provisions to take account of section 11 relating to the changes in Rent Allowances for tenants under Part VI contracts.

Local authorities are required to make their own rent allowance scheme conform with the model one under section 20 (1), Housing Finance Act 1973.

The abolition of the 25% mark up by section 11 (2) of this Act alters the basis of calculating the eligible rent for the allowances and consequently the schemes of the local authorities.   Since this abolition (subject to the transitional provisions in section 11 (3) (4) and (5)) operated immediately from 14th August 1974, local authorities were not given adequate time to vary their schemes.

Sub-paragraphs 4 (1) *and* (2)—accordingly provides that every local authority Rent Allowance Scheme shall be deemed to have been varied to take account of the 25% mark up until such time as local authorities have to vary their schemes to take account of the abolition of the qualified persons requirements, *i.e.* probably until 30th September 1974.

Sub-paragraph 4 (3)—provides that this deemed variation shall not require local authorities to send particulars of their scheme to their tenants.   Since they will in any event be required to do so when the qualified persons requirement is brought into force, it is felt too onerous to require them to do so also on the abolition of the 25% mark up.

Local authorities are therefore relieved of their obligation under section 25 (5) (*b*) of the Housing Finance Act 1972 to notify changes in their schemes to this limited extent.

Sub-paragraphs 4 (4) *and* (5)—empower a local authority to vary their schemes at any time to take account of the provisions of this Act but not so that the variations come into effect before the appointed day, *e.g.* probably 30th September 1974.

Paragraph 5—removes the obligation to consult the Advisory Committee on Rent Rebates and Rent Allowances for their advice under section 20 (3), Housing Finance Act 1972, in respect of any changes to be made to the model Rent Allowance Scheme contained in Schedules 3 and 4 in that Act.   The provisions relating to deductions from eligible rent for students should be referred to the Committee in particular.

However, the time scale given by the Government does not permit consultation with the Committee before the 30th September 1974 and in any event it would be difficult to convene it over the holiday period. Hence Parliament's authority was obtained to obviate the need to consult. This variation of the normal consultation procedure will be in force only for 3 months from the 14th August 1974, so that it will be in force again for any future deductions.

Paragraph 6—has similar effect in Scotland as paragraph 4 has in England and Wales.

SCHEDULE 4.

ENACTMENTS REPEALED

Part I of this Schedule lists those sections and Schedules which are repealed as at the 14th August 1974 of the Rent Act 1968, The Rent (Scotland) Act 1971, the Housing Finance Act 1972, the Housing (Financial Provisions) (Scotland) Act 1972 and the Furnished Lettings (Rent Allowances) Act 1973.

Part II of this Schedule lists those sections and Schedules of the Housing (Financial Provisions) (Scotland) Act 1973, the Housing Finance Act 1972 and the Furnished Lettings (Rent Allowances) Act 1973 which are repealed on the appointed day under the new provisions in this Act relating to Rent Allowances for furnished tenants (probably the 30th September 1974).

C.—TEXT OF THE RENT ACT 1974

ARRANGEMENT OF SECTIONS

RENT ACT 1974

ELIZABETH II

1974 Chapter 51

An Act to amend the Rent Act 1968 and the Rent (Scotland) Act 1971 and the provisions of Part II of the Housing Finance Act 1972 and of the Housing (Financial Provisions) (Scotland) Act 1972 relating to rent allowances, and for connected purposes.

[31st July 1974]

BE it enacted by the Queen's most Excellent Majesty, by and with the advice and consent of the Lords Spiritual and Temporal, and Commons, in this present Parliament assembled, and by the authority of the same, as follows:—

Modifications of Rent Act in relation to furnished and other tenancies

Extension of protection afforded to furnished tenancies.

1.—(1) On and after the commencement date,—

    (*a*) a tenancy of a dwelling-house shall no longer be prevented from being a protected tenancy for the purposes of the Rent Act by reason only that, under the tenancy, the dwelling-house is bona fide let at a rent which includes payments in respect of the use of furniture; and

    (*b*) subject to the following provisions of this Act, references in the Rent Act (and in any other enactment or instrument in which those expressions have the same meaning as in that Act) to a protected tenancy, a statutory tenancy or a regulated tenancy shall be construed accordingly.

(2) Any reference in this Act or the Rent Act to a protected furnished tenancy, a statutory furnished tenancy or a regulated furnished tenancy is a reference to a protected tenancy, a statutory tenancy or a regulated tenancy, as the case may be, under which the rent for the dwelling-house concerned includes such payments in respect of the use of furniture as, apart from subsection (1) above subsection (4)(*a*) below and the repeals effected by this Act, would prevent a tenancy of the dwelling-house at that rent from being a protected tenancy.

(3) Notwithstanding anything in section 7(1) of or Schedule 2 to the Rent Act (controlled and regulated tenancies) no protected furnished tenancy or statutory furnished tenancy shall be a controlled tenancy.

(4) In consequence of the provisions of this Act,—

    (*a*) in section 2(1)(*b*) of the Rent Act (exclusion from protection of tenancies where the rent includes payments in respect of

board, attendance or use of furniture) for the words
" attendance or use of furniture " there shall be substituted
the words " or attendance ";

(b) Schedule 3 to the Rent Act (grounds for possession) shall
have effect subject to the modifications in Part I of Schedule
1 to this Act;

(c) Parts IV, VIII and IX of the Rent Act 1968 shall have effect
subject to the amendments in Part II of that Schedule; and

(d) Parts IV, IX and X of the Rent (Scotland) Act 1971 shall
have effect subject to the amendments in Part III of that
Schedule.

Certain tenancies not to be protected.

2.—(1) In subsection (1) of section 2 of the Rent Act (tenancies
excepted from definition of " protected tenancy ") after paragraph
(b) there shall be inserted the following paragraphs:—

" (bb) the tenancy is granted to a person who is pursuing or
intends to pursue a course of study provided by a specified
educational institution and is so granted either by that
institution or by another specified institution or body of
persons; or

(bbb) the purpose of the tenancy is to confer on the tenant the
right to occupy the dwelling-house for a holiday; or ".

(2) After subsection (3) of section 2 of the Rent Act there shall
be added the following subsection:—

" (4) In paragraph (bb) of subsection (1) above " specified "
means specified, or of a class specified, for the purposes of that
paragraph by regulations made by the Secretary of State by
statutory instrument; and a statutory instrument containing
any such regulations shall be subject to annulment in pursuance
of a resolution of either House of Parliament."

(3) After section 5 of the Rent Act there shall be inserted the
section 5A set out in paragraph 1 or, as the case may require,
paragraph 2 of Part I of Schedule 2 to this Act and, accordingly,
in section 1(1) of the Rent Act (definition of protected tenancy) at
the end of paragraph (c) there shall be added the words—

" or

(d) by virtue of section 5A below, the tenancy has at all times
since it was granted been precluded from being a protected
tenancy ".

(4) Part IX of the Rent Act 1968 shall have effect subject to the
amendments in Part II of Schedule 2 to this Act and Part X of the
Rent (Scotland) Act 1971 shall have effect subject to the amendments
in Part III of that Schedule.

very of possession of dwelling-houses let on certain tenancies.

.—(1) In Part II of Schedule 3 to the Rent Act 1968 (Cases in which court must order possession of dwelling-house subject to regulated tenancy) the following Cases shall be inserted after Case 10:—

" Case 10A

Where a person (in this Case referred to as " the owner ") who acquired the dwelling-house or any interest therein with a view to occupying it as his residence at such time as he might retire from regular employment let it on a regulated tenancy before he has so retired and—

(a) not later than the relevant date the landlord gave notice in writing to the tenant that possession might be recovered under this Case; and

(b) the dwelling-house has not, since the commencement date, within the meaning of the Rent Act 1974, been let by the owner on a protected tenancy with respect to which the condition mentioned in paragraph (a) above was not satisfied; and

(c) the court is satisfied either than the owner has retired from regular employment and requires the dwelling-house as a residence or that the owner has died and the dwelling-house is required as a residence for a member of his family who was residing with him at the time of his death:

Provided that if the court is of the opinion that, notwithstanding that the condition in paragraph (a) or paragraph (b) above is not complied with, it is just and equitable to make an order for possession of the dwelling-house, the court may dispense with the requirements of either or both of those paragraphs, as the case may require.

Case 10B

Where the dwelling-house is let under a tenancy for a term of years certain not exceeding 8 months and—

(a) not later than the relevant date the landlord gave notice in writing to the tenant that possession might be recovered under this Case; and

(b) the dwelling-house was, at some time within the period of 12 months ending on the relevant date, occupied under a right to occupy it for a holiday;

and for the purposes of this Case a tenancy shall be treated as being for a term of years certain notwithstanding that it is liable to determination by re-entry or on the happening of any event other than the giving of notice by the landlord to determine the term.

Case 10C

Where the dwelling-house is let under a tenancy for a term of years certain not exceeding 12 months and—

(a) not later than the relevant date the landlord gave notice in writing to the tenant that possession might be recovered under this Case; and

(b) at some time within the period of 12 months ending on the relevant date, the dwelling-house was subject to such a tenancy as is referred to in section 2(1)(*bb*) of this Act;

and for the purposes of this Case a tenancy shall be treated as being for a term of years certain notwithstanding that it is liable to determination by re-entry or on the happening of any event other than the giving of notice by the landlord to determine the term."

(2) In Part II of Schedule 3 to the Rent (Scotland) Act 1971 (Cases in which court must order possession of dwelling-house subject to regulated tenancy) the following Cases shall be inserted after Case 11:—

" Case 11A

Where a person (in this Case referred to as " the owner ") who acquired the dwelling-house or any interest therein with a view to occupying it as his residence at such time as he might retire from regular employment let it on a regulated tenancy before he has so retired and—

(a) not later than the relevant date the landlord gave notice in writing to the tenant that possession might be recovered under this Case ; and

(b) the dwelling-house has not, since the commencement date, within the meaning of the Rent Act 1974, been let by the owner on a protected tenancy with respect to which the condition mentioned in paragraph (a) above was not satisfied; and

(c) the court is satisfied either that the owner has retired from regular employment and requires the dwelling-house as a residence or that the owner has died and the dwelling-house is required as a residence for a member of his family who was residing with him at the time of his death:

Provided that if the court is of the opinion that, notwithstanding that the condition in paragraph (*a*) or paragraph (*b*) above is not complied with, it is just and equitable to make an order for possession of the dwelling-house, the court may dispense with the requirements of either or both of those paragraphs, as the case may require.

Case 11*B*

Where the dwelling-house is let under a tenancy for a specified period not exceeding 8 months and—

(*a*) not later than the relevant date the landlord gave notice in writing to the tenant that possession might be recovered under this Case; and

(*b*) the dwelling-house was, at some time within the period of 12 months ending on the relevant date, occupied under a right to occupy it for a holiday;

and for the purposes of this Case a tenancy shall be treated as being for a specified period—

(i) of less than 8 months, if it is determinable at the option of the landlord (other than in the event of an irritancy being incurred) before the expiration of 8 months from the commencement of the period of the tenancy, and

(ii) of 8 months or more, if it confers on the tenant an option for renewal of the tenancy for a period which, together with the original period, amounts to 8 months or more, and it is not determinable as mentioned in paragraph (i) above.

Case 11*C*

Where the dwelling-house is let under a tenancy for a specified period not exceeding 12 months and—

(*a*) not later than the relevant date the landlord gave notice in writing to the tenant that possession might be recovered under this Case; and

(*b*) at some time within the period of 12 months ending on the relevant date the dwelling-house was subject to such a tenancy as is referred to in section 2(1)(*bb*) of this Act;

and for the purposes of this Case a tenancy shall be treated as being for a specified period—

(i) of less than 12 months, if it is determinable at the option of the landlord (other than in the event of an irritancy being incurred) before the expiration of 12 months from the commencement of the period of the tenancy, and

(ii) of 12 months or more, if it confers on the tenant an option for renewal of the tenancy for a period which, together with the original period, amounts to 12 months or more, and it is not determinable as mentioned in paragraph (i) above."

(3) At the end of Case 10 in Part II of Schedule 3 to the Rent Act 1968 and at the end of Case 11 in Part II of Schedule 3 to the Rent (Scotland) Act 1971 there shall be added the following proviso—

" Provided that if the court if of the opinion that, notwithstanding that the condition in paragraph (*a*) or paragraph (*b*) above is not complied with, it is just and equitable to make an order for possession of the dwelling-house, the court may dispense with the requirements of either or both of those paragraphs, as the case may require."

Advance Application for Registration of a new Rent.

4.—(1) At the beginning of subsection (3) of section 44 of the Rent Act 1968 (no application for registration of a new rent until three years after a previous registration) there shall be inserted the words " Subject to subsection (3A) below " and at the end of that subsection there shall be added the following subsection:—

" (3A) Notwithstanding anything in subsection (3) above, an application such as is mentioned in that subsection which is made by the landlord alone and is so made within the last three months of the period of three years referred to in that subsection may be entertained notwithstanding that that period has not expired."

(2) At the beginning of subsection (1) of section 48 of that Act (effect of registration of rent) there shall be inserted the words " Subject to subsection (1A) below " and at the end of that subsection there shall be added the following subsection:—

" (1A) Where, by virtue of subsection (3A) of section 44 above, an application is made before the expiry of the period of three years referred to in subsection (3) of that section, subsection (1) above shall have effect as if for the reference to the date of the application there were substituted a reference to the first day after the expiry of that period of three years."

(3) At the beginning of subsection (3) of section 40 of the Rent (Scotland) Act 1971 (no application for registration of a new rent until three years after a previous registration) there shall be inserted

the words " Subject to subsection (3A) below " and at the end of
that subsection there shall be added the following subsection:—

> " (3A) An application such as is mentioned in subsection
> (3) above which is made by the landlord alone and is so made
> within the last three months of the period of three years referred
> to in that subsection may be entertained before the expiry of
> that period, notwithstanding that the application is not made
> upon any of the grounds mentioned in that subsection."

(4) At the beginning of subsection (1) of section 44 of the said
Act of 1971 (effect of registration of rent) there shall be inserted
the words " Subject to subsection (1A) below " and at the end of
that subsection there shall be added the following subsection:—

> " (1A) Where, by virtue of subsection (3A) of section 40
> above, an application is made before the expiry of the period
> of three years referred to in subsection (3) of that section,
> subsection (1) above shall have effect as if for the reference to
> the date of the application there were substituted a reference
> to the first day after the expiry of that period of three years."

Transitional provisions affecting furnished lettings which become furnished tenancies.

5.—(1) In any case where—

> (a) immediately before the commencement date a dwelling is
>   subject to a furnished letting and a rent is registered for
>   that dwelling under the relevant Part of the Rent Act, and
> (b) on the commencement date that furnished letting becomes
>   a protected furnished tenancy by virtue of section 1 above,

the amount which is so registered under the relevant Part of the
Rent Act shall be deemed to be registered under Part IV of that
Act as the rent for the dwelling-house which is let on that tenancy,
and that registration shall be deemed to take effect on the commencement date.

(2) Section 44(3) of the Rent Act 1968 or, as the case may require,
section 40(3) of the Rent (Scotland) Act 1971 (no application for
registration of a different rent to be made within 3 years of the last
registration) shall not apply to an application for the registration
under Part IV of the Rent Act of a rent different from that which is
deemed to be registered as mentioned in subsection (1) above.

(3) The reference in section 45(1)(b) of the Rent Act 1968 or, as
the case may require, section 41(1)(b) of the Rent (Scotland) Act
1971 (certificates of fair rent) to a rent being registered for a dwelling-
house does not include a rent which is deemed to be registered as
mentioned in subsection (1) above.

(4) In any case where—

(a) before the commencement date a notice to quit had been served in respect of a dwelling to which a furnished letting then related, and

(b) the period at the end of which that notice to quit takes effect had, before the commencement date, been extended under the relevant Part of the Rent Act, and

(c) that period has not expired before the commencement date, and

(d) on the commencement date the furnished letting becomes a protected furnished tenancy by virtue of section 1 above,

the notice to quit shall take effect on the day following the commencement date (whenever it would otherwise take effect) and, accordingly, on that day the protected furnished tenancy shall become a statutory furnished tenancy.

Furnished lettings (England and Wales)

Furnished lettings: increase in rateable value limits.

6. In section 71 of the Rent Act 1968 (dwellings to which Part VI applies) for subsection (1) there shall be substituted the following subsections:—

" (1) Subject to any provision made by an order under subsection (2) below, where the appropriate day in relation to any dwelling fell before 1st April 1973, this Part of this Act applies to the dwelling if—

(a) it had on the appropriate day a rateable value not exceeding, if it is in Greater London, £400, or, if it is elsewhere, £200; or

(b) it had on 1st April 1973 a rateable value not exceeding, if it is in Greater London, £1500, or, if it is elsewhere, £750.

(1A) Subject to any provision made by an order under subsection (2) below, where the appropriate day in relation to any dwelling fell or falls on or after 1st April 1973, this Part of this Act applies to the dwelling if it has or had on the appropriate day a rateable value not exceeding, if it is in Greater London, £1500, or, if it is elsewhere, £750."

Furnished lettings: amendments relating to control and registration of rents.

7.—(1) In section 73(1) of the Rent Act 1968 (powers of rent tribunals on reference of Part VI contracts) in paragraph (b) (power to reduce the rent to such sum as the tribunal thinks reasonable) after the word " reduce " there shall be inserted the words " or increase " and accordingly the following provisions of that Act shall cease to have effect, namely,—

    (*a*) section 73(3) (under which the tribunal could, in respect of certain long-standing contracts, approve a rent higher than that payable under the contract); and

    (*b*) section 75(2) (under which, on a reference made after a rent had been registered, the tribunal had power to increase the rent payable).

(2) For subsection (5) of section 73 of that Act (the tribunal need not entertain any reference made by a lessee or lessor alone if they are satisfied that the reference is frivolous or vexatious) there shall be substituted the following subsection:—

    " (5) Where the rent under a Part VI contract has been registered under section 74 below, a rent tribunal shall not be required to entertain a reference, made otherwise than by the lessor and the lessee jointly, for the registration of a different rent for the dwelling concerned before the expiry of the period of 3 years beginning on the date on which the rent was last considered by the tribunal, except on the ground that, since that date, there has been such a change in the condition of the dwelling, the furniture or services provided, the terms of the contract or any other circumstances taken into consideration when the rent was last considered as to make the registered rent no longer a reasonable rent."

(3) In section 74 of that Act (register of rents under Part VI contracts) after subsection (2) there shall be inserted the following subsection:—

    " (2A) Where any rates in respect of a dwelling are borne by the lessor or any person having any title superior to that of the lessor, the amount to be entered in the register under this section as the rent payable for the dwelling shall be the same as if the rates were not so borne; but the fact that they are so borne shall be noted in the register."

(4) In section 75(1) of that Act (reconsideration of rent after registration) after the words " section 74 above " there shall be inserted the words " then, subject to section 73(5) above " and the words " on the ground of change of circumstances " shall be omitted.

(5) In section 76 of that Act (effect of registration of rent) after subsection (1) there shall be added the following subsection:—

    " (1A) Where subsection (2A) of section 74 above applies, the amount entered in the register under that section shall be treated for the purposes of this section as increased for any rental period by the amount of the rates for that period, ascertained in accordance with Schedule 4 to this Act."

(6) In section 84(1) of that Act (interpretation of Part VI) after the definition of " register " there shall be inserted the following definition:—

" ' rental period ' means a period in respect of which a payment of rent falls to be made ".

Furnished lettings: amendments relating to security of tenure.

8.—(1) In section 78(1) of the Rent Act 1968 (application by lessee to rent tribunal for extension of period before notice to quit takes effect) paragraph (c) (no application may be made if the rent tribunal has previously granted an extension of less than six months) shall be omitted.

(2) In section 80 of that Act (reduction of period of notice on account of lessee's default) at the end of paragraph (c) of subsection (2) there shall be added the words " or

(d) that the condition of any furniture provided for the use of the lessee under the contract has deteriorated owing to any ill-treatment by the lessee or any person residing or lodging with him ".

Furnished lettings (Scotland)

Furnished lettings: amendments relating to control and registration of rents.

9.—(1) In section 88(1) of the Rent (Scotland) Act 1971 (powers of rent tribunals on reference of Part VII contracts) in paragraph (b) (power to reduce the rent to such sum as the tribunal thinks reasonable) after the word " reduce " there shall be inserted the words " or increase ", and accordingly section 90(2) of that Act (under which, on a reference made after a rent had been registered, the tribunal had power to increase the rent payable) shall cease to have effect.

(2) For subsection (4) of section 88 of that Act (the tribunal need not entertain any reference made by a lessee or lessor alone if they are satisfied that the reference is frivolous or vexatious) there shall be substituted the following subsection:—

" (4) Where the rent under a Part VII contract has been registered under section 89 below, a rent tribunal shall not be required to entertain a reference, made otherwise than by the lessor and the lessee jointly, for the registration of a different rent for the dwelling-house concerned before the expiry of the period of 3 years beginning on the date on which the rent was last considered by the tribunal, except on the ground that, since that date, there has been such a change in the condition of the dwelling-house, the furniture or services provided, the terms of the contract or any other circumstances taken into consideration when the rent was last considered as to make the registered rent no longer a reasonable rent."

(3) In section 89 of that Act (register of rents under Part VII contracts) after subsection (2) there shall be inserted the following subsection:—

" (2A) Where any rates in respect of a dwelling-house are borne by the lessor, the amount to be entered in the register under this section as the rent payable for the dwelling-house shall be the same as if the rates were not so borne; but the fact that they are so borne shall be noted in the register."

(4) In section 90(1) of that Act (reconsideration of rent after registration) after the words " section 89 above " there shall be inserted the words " then, subject to section 88(4) above " and the words " on the ground of change of circumstances " shall be omitted.

(5) In section 91 of that Act (effect of registration of rent) after subsection (1) there shall be added the following subsection:—

" (1A) Where subsection (2A) of section 89 above applies, the amount entered in the register under that section shall be treated for the purposes of this section as increased for any rental period by the amount of the rates for that period, ascertained in accordance with Schedule 4 to this Act."

(6) In section 100(1) of that Act (interpretation of Part VII) after the definition of " register " there shall be inserted the following definition:—

" ' rental period ' means a period in respect of which a payment of rent falls to be made ".

Furnished lettings: amendments relating to security of tenure.

10.—(1) In section 93(1) of the Rent (Scotland) Act 1971 (application by lessee to rent tribunal for extension of period before notice to quit takes effect) paragraph (c) (no application may be made if the rent tribunal has previously granted an extension of less than six months) shall be omitted.

(2) In section 95 of that Act (reduction of period of notice on account of lessee's default) at the end of paragraph (c) of subsection (2) there shall be added the words " or

(d) that the condition of any furniture provided for the use of the lessee under the contract has deteriorated owing to any ill-treatment by the lessee or any person residing or lodging with him ".

Supplementary

Rent Allowances.

11.—(1) On and after such day as the Secretary of State may by order made by statutory instrument appoint, so much of Part II of the Housing Finance Act 1972 (rent rebates and rent allowances) as requires that, in order to qualify for an allowance, a person occupying a dwelling under a Part VI letting must be a qualified person, within the meaning of section 19(12) of that Act, shall cease to have effect.

(2) The proviso to subsection (1) of section 25 of the Housing Finance Act 1972 (which, in the case of certain furnished lettings, determines the rent which is eligible to be met by a rebate or an allowance for the purposes of Schedule 3 to that Act) shall cease to have effect on the commencement date.

(3) Notwithstanding anything in subsection (2) above, in the case of a person who immediately before the commencement date was a tenant under a Part VI letting, the provisions of subsection (4) below shall apply if, for an allowance period which was current on or ended immediately before the commencement date, the tenant was entitled to an allowance towards the rent payable under the Part VI letting and, in calculating that allowance for the last week of that period which ended before the commencement date, the rent which, for the purposes of Schedule 3 to the Housing Finance Act 1972, was eligible to be met by a rebate or an allowance was that determined under paragraph (*a*) of the proviso to section 25(1) of that Act (the occupational element of the rent or of the residue of the rent plus 25 per cent.).

(4) If, by virtue of subsection (3) above, this subsection applies in relation to a tenant, then, subject to subsection (5) below, on and after the commencement date, if and so long as—

(*a*) the tenant continues to occupy as his home the dwelling to which, immediately before that date, the Part VI letting referred to in subsection (3) above applied, and

(*b*) the tenant continues to be entitled to an allowance towards the rent payable by him for that dwelling, and

(*c*) that rent continues to include payment for the use of furniture,

the rent which, for the purposes of Schedule 3 to the Housing Finance Act 1972, is eligible to be met by a rebate or an allowance shall, in his case, be the amount of the rent which was so eligible for the week mentioned in subsection (3) above (in this section referred to as " the former eligible rent ").

(5) For any week of an allowance period when, apart from this subsection, subsection (4) above would apply in relation to a tenant, that subsection shall cease to apply if—

> (a) the amount determined under section 25(1) of the Housing Finance Act 1972 as the rent which is eligible to be met by a rebate or an allowance exceeds the former eligible rent, or

> (b) the rent recoverable from the tenant, exclusive of any part thereof attributable to rates, is less than the former eligible rent, or

> (c) part of the dwelling is sub-let and the former eligible rent either did not take account of the occupational element of any rent payable by a sub-tenant or took account of such an element which is less than the occupational element of the rent payable for that week by the sub-tenant,

and, accordingly, from the beginning of that week the rent which is eligible to be met by a rebate or an allowance shall be that determined as mentioned in paragraph (a) above.

(6) In subsection (1) of section 25 of the Housing Finance Act 1972 after the words " of the rent " there shall be inserted, in substitution for the words there inserted by paragraph 17 of Schedule 1 to the Furnished Lettings (Rent Allowances) Act 1973, the words " (or if, in the case of an allowance, any amount falls to be deducted by virtue of paragraph 14 of Schedule 4 to this Act, the occupational element of the residue of the rent remaining after deducting those amounts) ".

(7) Subsections (2) and (3) of the said section 25 shall be amended as follows:—

> (a) at the end of subsection (2) there shall be added the words " and
>> (c) less, in the case of an allowance, any amount which, in the case of the tenant concerned, is prescribed as a deduction by virtue of paragraph (c) of subsection (3) below "; and

> (b) at the end of subsection (3) there shall be added the words " and
>> (c) prescribe deductions from rent for the purposes of subsection (2)(c) above in the case of tenants of such descriptions as may be specified in the regulations who are for the time being in receipt of awards or grants under any provision of sections 1 to 3 of the Education Act 1962 or any other award or grant which is paid out of money provided by Parliament and is determined by the Secretary of State to be an analogous award or grant,

and different provision may be made by virtue of paragraph (c) above in relation to different periods and different classes of awards or grants ".

(8) In subsection (1) of section 26 of the Housing Finance Act 1972 (interpretation of Part II) in the definition of " tenant " after paragraph (c) there shall be inserted the following paragraph:—

" (d) a person who is treated as a private tenant under a Part VI letting by virtue of subsection (8A) of section 19 of this Act ".

(9) The said section 26 shall apply in relation to subsections (1) to (5) above as if those subsections were included in Part II of the Housing Finance Act 1972 and, without prejudice to the application of that section, the reference in subsection (3) above to a tenant under a Part VI letting includes a reference to a person who is treated as if he were a private tenant under a Part VI letting by virtue of section 19(8A) of that Act and any reference in that subsection or subsection (4) above to a Part VI letting means, in relation to a person who is so treated, the letting referred to in the said section 19(8A).

Rent Allowances in Scotland.

12.—(1) On and after such day as the Secretary of State may by order made by statutory instrument appoint, so much of section 16 of the Act of 1972 (rent allowances) as requires that, for certain persons to be or to be treated as private tenants, they must be qualified persons within the meaning of subsection (8) of that section, shall cease to have effect.

(2) In paragraph 15(1)(g)(ii) of Schedule 3 to the Act of 1972 (which provides that in ascertaining the amount of an allowance in respect of a furnished letting a certain amount of rent payable is to be disregarded), the words " 125 per cent. of " shall cease to have effect on the commencement date.

(3) Notwithstanding anything in subsection (2) above, in the case of a person who immediately before the commencement date was a tenant of a dwelling-house under a furnished letting, the provisions of subsection (4) below shall apply if, for an allowance period which was current on or ended immediately before that date, the tenant was entitled to an allowance towards the rent payable under the furnished letting which was calculated, for the last week of that period which ended before that date, by reference to an amount of rent which, after making the deduction (if any) required by head (i) of paragraph 15(1)(g) of Schedule 3 to the Act of 1972, was more than the estimated fair rent referred to in head (ii) of that paragraph but not more than 125 per cent. of that estimated fair rent.

(4) If, by virtue of subsection (3) above, this subsection applies in relation to a tenant, then, if and so long as he continues on and after the commencement date to be—

(*a*) a tenant of the same dwelling-house under the same letting (whether or not it continues to be a furnished letting), and

(*b*) entitled to an allowance towards the rent under the letting concerned,

the allowance shall be calculated by reference to the amount of rent referred to in subsection (3) above until—

(i) the rent recoverable from the tenant for any week of an allowance period is less than the amount referred to in that subsection, or

(ii) the amount of rent by reference to which, but for this subsection, the allowance for any such week would be calculated is higher than the amount referred to in subsection (3) above,

whichever is the earlier; and as from the beginning of that week the allowance shall be calculated by reference to the amount of rent to which an authority would be entitled to have regard but for this subsection.

(5) Paragraph 17 of Schedule 2 to the Act of 1972 shall be amended as follows—

(*a*) in sub-paragraph (1) for the words " sub-paragraph (2) below " there shall be substituted the words " the following provisions of this paragraph ";

(*b*) at the end there shall be added the following sub-paragraphs—

" (3) It shall be the duty of every authority, for the purpose of computing the amount of an allowance towards the rent payable by tenants of such classes as may be prescribed who are for the time being in receipt of—

(*a*) an award or grant, being a bursary, scholarship or allowance granted under section 49(1) or 75(*f*) of the Education (Scotland) Act 1962 or

(*b*) any other award or grant which is paid out of money provided by Parliament and is determined by the Secretary of State to be analogous to any such bursary, scholarship or allowance,

to treat the rent as reduced by such amount as may be prescribed.

(4) In sub-paragraph (3) above " prescribed " means prescribed by regulations made by the Secretary of State by statutory instrument which shall be subject to annulment in pursuance of a resolution of either House of Parliament.

(5) Regulations under this paragraph may make different provision in relation to different periods and different classes of awards or grants."

(6) In this section " the Act of 1972 " means the Housing (Financial Provisions) (Scotland) Act 1972; and section 22 of the Act of 1972 (interpretation of Part II of that Act) shall apply in relation to this section as if it were included in that Part.

Effect on furnished sub-tenancy of determination of superior unfurnished tenancy.

13.—(1) Without prejudice to the operation of section 1(1) above if, in a case where subsection (2) of section 18 of the Rent Act 1968 or, as the case may require, section 17 of the Rent (Scotland) Act 1971 applies (effect on sub-tenancies of determination of superior tenancy), the relevant conditions are fulfilled, the terms on which the sub-tenant is, by virtue of that subsection, deemed to become the tenant of the landlord shall not include any terms as to the provision by the landlord of furniture or services.

(2) The relevant conditions referred to in subsection (1) above are—

(*a*) that the tenancy or statutory tenancy which is determined as mentioned in the said section 18(2) or, as the case may require, 17(2) was neither a protected furnished tenancy nor a statutory furnished tenancy; and

(*b*) that, immediately before the determination of that tenancy or statutory tenancy, the sub-tenant referred to in that section was the tenant under a protected furnished tenancy or a statutory furnished tenancy; and

(*c*) that the landlord, within the period of 6 weeks beginning with the day on which the tenancy or statutory tenancy referred to in that section is determined, serves notice on the sub-tenant that this section is to apply to his tenancy or statutory tenancy.

Power of Court in action for Possession to reduce period of Notice to Quit.

14.—(1) After section 80 of the Rent Act 1968 there shall be inserted the following section:—

" Power of county court, in action for possession, to reduce period of notice to quit.

80A. In any case where—

    (*a*) a notice to quit a dwelling which is the subject of a Part VI contract has been served, and

    (*b*) the period at the end of which the notice to quit takes effect is for the time being extended by virtue of section 77 or section 78 above, and

    (*c*) at some time during that period the lessor institutes proceedings in the county court for the recovery of possession of the dwelling, and

    (*d*) in those proceedings the county court is satisfied that any of paragraphs (*a*) to (*d*) of section 80(2) above applies,

the court may direct that the period referred to in paragraph (*b*) above shall be reduced so as to end at a date specified in the direction."

(2) At the end of subsection (3) of section 106 of that Act (rules as to procedure) there shall be added the words " and section 80A."

(3) After section 95 of the Rent (Scotland) Act 1971 there shall be inserted the following section:—

" Power of sheriff, in action for possession, to reduce period of notice to quit.

95A. In any case where—

    (*a*) a notice to quit a dwelling-house which is the subject of a Part VII contract has been served, and

    (*b*) the period at the end of which the notice to quit takes effect is for the time being extended by virtue of section 92 or section 93 above, and

    (*c*) at some time during that period the lessor institutes proceedings before the sheriff for possession of the dwelling-house, and

    (*d*) in those proceedings the sheriff is satisfied that any of paragraphs (*a*) to (*d*) of section 95(2) above applies,

the sheriff may direct that the period referred to in paragraph (*b*) above shall be reduced so as to end at a date specified in the direction."

Interpretation.

15.—(1) In this Act—

"commencement date" means the date on which this Act comes into operation;

"dwelling", in relation to a furnished letting, means a house or part of a house;

"furnished letting" means a Part VI contract as defined in section 70(6) of the Rent Act 1968 or, as the case may require, a Part VII contract, as defined in section 85(5) of the Rent (Scotland) Act 1971;

"protected furnished tenancy", "regulated furnished tenancy" and "statutory furnished tenancy" shall be construed in accordance with section 1(2) above;

"the Rent Act" means, in relation to England and Wales, the Rent Act 1968 and, in relation to Scotland, the Rent (Scotland) Act 1971;

"the relevant Part of the Rent Act" means Part VI of the Rent Act 1968 or, as the case may require, Part VII of the Rent (Scotland) Act 1971; and

"services" has the same meaning as in the relevant Part of the Rent Act.

(2) Without prejudice to subsection (1) above, section 113(1) of the Rent Act 1968 or, as the case may require, section 133(1) of the Rent (Scotland) Act 1971 (interpretation) shall apply for the purposes of this Act other than sections 11 and 12 above as it applies for the purposes of that Act.

(3) Except in so far as the context otherwise requires, any reference in this Act to any other enactment shall be taken as referring to that enactment as amended by or under any other enactment, including this Act.

Transitional provisions and repeals.

16.—(1) The transitional provisions in Schedule 3 to this Act shall have effect, notwithstanding anything in the preceding provisions of this Act.

(2) The enactments specified in Schedule 4 to this Act are hereby repealed to the extent specified in the third column of that Schedule but, in the case of the enactments specified in Part II of that Schedule, only with effect from the day appointed for the purposes of subsection (1) of sections 11 and 12 above.

Short title, citation, application, commencement and extent.

17.—(1) This Act may be cited as the Rent Act 1974.

(2) This Act and the Rent Act 1968 may be cited together as the Rent Acts 1968 and 1974.

(3) This Act and the Rent (Scotland) Acts 1971 and 1972 may be cited together as the Rent (Scotland) Acts 1971 to 1974.

(4) In section 115 of the Rent Act 1968 (application to Isles of Scilly)—

> (a) in subsection (1), after the words " this Act " there shall be inserted the words " and the Rent Act 1974 ";
>
> (b) at the end of paragraph (e) of subsection (2) there shall be inserted the words " and
>
>> (f) any provision of this Act which is derived from the Rent Act 1974, other than a provision of Part VI of this Act, and any other provision of the Rent Act 1974 ".

(5) This Act shall come into operation at the expiry of the period of two weeks beginning with the date on which it is passed.

(6) Sections 3(1), 4(1) and (2), 6, 7, 8, 11 and 14(1) and (2) of this Act and Part II of Schedules 1 and 2 to this Act do not extend to Scotland and sections 3(2), 4(3) and (4), 9, 10, 12 and 14(3) of this Act and Part III of Schedules 1 and 2 to this Act extend to Scotland only.

(7) This Act does not extend to Northern Ireland.

SCHEDULES

SCHEDULE 1

Section 1.

CONSEQUENTIAL AMENDMENTS OF RENT ACT

PART I

AMENDMENTS OF SCHEDULE 3 TO RENT ACT

1. After Case 3 there shall be inserted the following Case:—

" *Case* 3A

Where the condition of any furniture provided for use under the tenancy has, in the opinion of the court, deteriorated owing to ill-treatment by the tenant or any person residing or lodging with him or any sub-tenant of his and, in the case of any ill-treatment by a person lodging with the tenant or a sub-tenant of his, where the court is satisfied that the tenant has not, before the making of the order in question, taken such steps as he ought reasonably to have taken for the removal of the lodger or sub-tenant, as the case may be."

2. In the application of Case 5 (assignment or subletting by tenant without landlord's consent) to a regulated furnished tenancy, for the reference to 8th December 1965 there shall be substituted a reference to the commencement date.

3. In the application of Case 8 (dwelling-house required for landlord or a member of his family) to a dwelling-house subject to a regulated furnished tenancy, for the reference to 23rd March 1965 there shall be substituted a reference to 24th May 1974.

4.—(1) In Case 9 (overcharging by tenant of his own sub-tenant)—

(a) after the words " by the tenant " there shall be inserted " (*a*) " and the word " also " shall be omitted; and

(b) subject to sub-paragraph (2) below, at the end of the Case there shall be added the words " or

(b) for any sublet part of the dwelling-house which is subject to a contract to which Part VI of this Act applies is or was in excess of the maximum (if any) which it is lawful for the lessor, within the meaning of that Part, to require or receive having regard to the provisions of that Part ".

(2) In the application of sub-paragraph (1)(*b*) above to Scotland for the words " Part VI " there shall be substituted the words " Part VII ".

5.—(1) In the application of Case 10 in Schedule 3 to the Rent Act 1968 or, as the case may be, Case 11 in Schedule 3 to the Rent (Scotland) Act 1971 (right of owner-occupier to regain possession) to a dwelling-house subject to a regulated furnished tenancy, for the reference to 8th December 1965 there shall be substituted a reference to the commencement date.

(2) For the purposes of each of the Cases referred to in sub-paragraph (1) above, the giving of a notice before the commencement date under section 79 of the Rent Act 1968 or, as the case may be, section 94 of the Rent (Scotland) Act 1971 (notice by owner-occupier to person taking up furnished letting) shall be treated in the case of a regulated furnished tenancy as compliance with paragraph (*a*) of the Case in question.

6. In Part III, in paragraph 2 (definition of relevant date) at the beginning of sub-paragraph (*a*) there shall be inserted the words " except in the case of a regulated furnished tenancy ", and after that sub-paragraph there shall be inserted the following sub-paragraph:—

" (*aa*) in the case of a regulated furnished tenancy, if the tenancy or, in the case of a statutory furnished tenancy, the previous contractual tenancy was created before the commencement date, within the meaning of the Rent Act 1974, the relevant date means the date on which expires the period of six months beginning on that commencement date; and ".

7. In Part IV, in paragraph 3 (meaning of suitable alternative accommodation) the following words shall be added at the end of sub-paragraph (1):—

" and that if any furniture was provided for use under the protected or statutory tenancy in question, furniture is provided for use in the accommodation which is either similar to that so provided or is reasonably suitable to the needs of the tenant and his family ".

PART II

AMENDMENTS OF PARTS IV, VIII AND IX OF RENT ACT 1968

8. In section 44(3) (circumstances in which applications may be made for variation of registered rent) after the words " terms of the tenancy " there shall be inserted the words " the quantity, quality or condition of any furniture provided for use under the tenancy (deterioration by fair wear and tear excluded) ".

9.—(1) In section 46 (determination of fair rent) in subsection (1) (circumstances to be considered in determining fair rent) for the words from " age " to the end of the subsection there shall be substituted the words " age, character, locality and state of repair of the dwelling-house and, if any furniture is provided for use under the tenancy, to the quantity, quality and condition of the furniture ".

(2) At the end of subsection (3) of that section (factors to be disregarded) there shall be inserted the words " and

    (c) if any furniture is provided for use under the regulated tenancy, any improvement to the furniture by the tenant under the regulated tenancy or any predecessor in title of his or as the case may be any deterioration in the condition of the furniture due to any ill-treatment by the tenant, any person residing or lodging with him, or any sub-tenant of his ".

10. In the application of sections 93 to 95 (mortgages) to a dwelling-house subject to a regulated tenancy which is a regulated furnished tenancy, for any reference to 8th December 1965 there shall be substituted a reference to the commencement date.

11. In section 103(1)(b) (certain sublettings not to exclude any part of the lessor's premises from protection) for the words " attendance or use of furniture " there shall be substituted the words " or attendance ".

12. In section 105(1) (county court jurisdiction to determine certain questions) after paragraph (d) there shall be inserted the words " or

    (e) as to whether a protected, statutory or regulated tenancy is a protected, statutory or regulated furnished tenancy ".

13. In section 106(1) (rules as to procedure) after the words " this Act " there shall be inserted the words " or the Rent Act 1974 ".

14. In section 107 (powers of local authorities for the purposes of giving information) in subsection (1)(a)(iii) after the words " this Act " there shall be inserted the words " and the Rent Act 1974 ".

15.—(1) In Schedule 6, in paragraph 10 (procedure on application for registration of rent supported by certificate of fair rent) in sub-paragraph (1) after the words " may be, whether " there shall be inserted " (a) " and at the end of the sub-paragraph there shall be inserted the words " and

    (*b*) if any furniture is or is to be provided for use under a
regulated tenancy of the dwelling-house, the quantity,
quality and condition of the furniture in the dwelling-house
accords with the prescribed particulars contained in the
application for the certificate ".

(2) In sub-paragraph (2) of that paragraph after the words " may
be, that " there shall be inserted " (*a*) " and after the words " of the
certificate " there shall be inserted the words " and

    (*b*) if any furniture is or is to be provided for use under a
regulated tenancy of the dwelling-house, the quantity,
quality and condition of the furniture in the dwelling-
house accords with the prescribed particulars contained in
the application for the certificate ".

16.   In Schedule 7, in paragraph 1 (form and content of application for certificate of fair rent) the word " and " at the end of sub-
paragraph (*b*) shall be omitted and at the end of the paragraph there
shall be inserted the words " and

    (*d*) if any furniture is to be provided for use under a regulated
tenancy of the dwelling-house, must contain the prescribed
particulars with regard to any such furniture ".

PART III

AMENDMENTS OF PARTS IV, IX AND X OF RENT (SCOTLAND) ACT 1971

17.   In section 40(3) (circumstances in which applications may
be made for variation of registered rent) after the words " terms of
the tenancy " there shall be inserted the words " the quantity,
quality or condition of any furniture provided for use under the
tenancy (excluding any deterioration in that furniture due to fair
wear and tear) ".

18.—(1) In section 42 (determination of fair rent) in subsection
(1) (circumstances to be considered in determining fair rent) for
the words from " age " to the end of the subsection there shall be
substituted the words " age, character, locality and state of repair
of the dwelling-house and, if any furniture is provided for use
under the tenancy, to the quantity, quality and condition of the
furniture ".

(2) In subsection (3) of that section (factors to be disregarded)—

    (*a*) in paragraph (*b*), after the word " improvement " there
shall be inserted the words " (including any improvement to
the furniture provided for use under the tenancy) ";

(*b*) at the end there shall be inserted the words " and

(*c*) if any furniture is provided for use under the regulated tenancy, any deterioration in the condition of the furniture due to any ill-treatment by the tenant, any person residing or lodging with him, or any sub-tenant of his ".

19.   In the application of sections 110 to 112 (heritable securities) to a dwelling-house subject to a regulated tenancy which is a regulated furnished tenancy, for any reference to 8th December 1965 there shall be substituted a reference to the commencement date.

20.   In section 120(1)(*b*) (certain sublettings not to exclude any part of the lessor's premises from protection) for the words " attendance or use of furniture " there shall be substituted the words " or attendance ".

21.   In section 122(1) (jurisdiction) in paragraph (*a*) after the words " this Act " there shall be inserted the words " or the Rent Act 1974 ".

22.   In section 124 (rules as to procedure) after the words " this Act " there shall be inserted the words " or the Rent Act 1974 ".

23.   In section 125 (powers of local authorities for the purposes of giving information) in subsection (1)(*a*) after the word " 1965 " there shall be inserted the word " and " and after the word " 1972 " there shall be inserted the words " and the Rent Act 1974 ".

24.—(1) In Schedule 6, in paragraph 10 (procedure on application for registration of rent supported by certificate of fair rent) in sub-paragraph (1) after the words " may be, whether " there shall be inserted " (*a*) " and at the end of the sub-paragraph there shall be inserted the words " and

(*b*) if any furniture is or is to be provided for use under a regulated tenancy of the dwelling-house, the quantity, quality and condition of the furniture in the dwelling-house accords with the prescribed particulars contained in the application for the certificate ".

(2) In sub-paragraph (2) of that paragraph after the words " may be, that " there shall be inserted " (*a*) " and after the words " of the certificate " there shall be inserted the words " and

(*b*) if any furniture is or is to be provided for use under a regulated tenancy of the dwelling-house, the quantity, quality and condition of the furniture in the dwelling-house accords with the prescribed particulars contained in the application for the certificate ".

25.   In Schedule 7, in paragraph 1 (form and content of application for certificate of fair rent) the word " and " at the end of sub-paragraph (b) shall be omitted and at the end of the paragraph there shall be inserted the words " and

(d) if any furniture is to be provided for use under a regulated tenancy of the dwelling-house, must contain the prescribed particulars with regard to any such furniture ".

SCHEDULE 2

Section 2.

TENANCIES GRANTED BY RESIDENT LANDLORDS

PART I

SECTION TO BE INSERTED AFTER SECTION 5 OF THE RENT ACT

1. The following section shall be inserted after section 5 of the Rent Act 1968:—

" No
protected
tenancy
in certain
cases where
landlord's
interest
belongs to
resident
landlord.

5A.—(1) Subject to subsection (5) below, a tenancy of a dwelling-house which is granted on or after the commencement date, within the meaning of the Rent Act 1974, shall not be a protected tenancy at any time if—

(a) the dwelling-house forms part only of a building and that building is not a purpose-built block of flats; and

(b) the tenancy was granted by a person who, at the time that he granted it, occupied as his residence another dwelling-house which also forms part of that building; and

(c) subject to subsection (2) below, at all times since the tenancy was granted, the interest of the landlord under the tenancy has belonged to a person who, at the time he owned that interest, occupied as his residence another dwelling-house which also formed part of that building.

(2) In determining whether the condition in paragraph (c) of subsection (1) above is at any time fulfilled with respect to a tenancy, there shall be disregarded—

(a) any period of not more than 14 days beginning with the date on which the interest of the landlord under the tenancy becomes vested at law and in equity in an individual who, during that period, does not occupy as his residence another dwelling-house which forms part of the building concerned;

(b) if, within a period falling within paragraph (a) above, the individual concerned notifies the tenant in writing of his intention to occupy as his residence another such dwelling-house as is referred to in that paragraph, the period beginning with the date on which the interest of the landlord under the tenancy becomes vested in that individual as mentioned in that paragraph and ending—

  (i) at the expiry of the period of 6 months beginning on that date, or

  (ii) on the date on which that interest ceases to be so vested, or

  (iii) on the date on which the condition in subsection (1)(*c*) above again applies,

whichever is the earlier; and

(*c*) any period of not more than 12 months beginning with the date on which the interest of the landlord under the tenancy becomes, and during which it remains, vested—

  (i) in the personal representatives of a deceased person acting in that capacity; or

  (ii) in trustees as such; or

  (iii) by virtue of section 9 of the Administration of Estates Act 1925, in the Probate Judge, within the meaning of that Act.

(3) During any period when—

(*a*) the interest of the landlord under the tenancy referred to in subsection (1) above is vested in trustees as such, and

(*b*) that interest is or, if it is held on trust for sale, the proceeds of its sale are held on trust for any person who occupies as his residence a dwelling-house which forms part of the building referred to in paragraph (*a*) of that subsection,

the condition in paragraph (*c*) of that subsection shall be deemed to be fulfilled and, accordingly, no part of that period shall be disregarded by virtue of subsection (2) above.

(4) Throughout any period which, by virtue of subsection (2) above, falls to be disregarded for the purpose of determining whether the condition in subsection (1)(*c*) above is fulfilled with respect to a tenancy,

no order shall be made for possession of the dwelling-house subject to that tenancy, other than an order which might be made if that tenancy were or, as the case may be, had been a regulated tenancy.

(5) This section does not apply to a tenancy of a dwelling-house which forms part of a building if—

(a) the tenancy is granted to a person who, immediately before it was granted, was a protected or statutory tenant of that dwelling-house or of any other dwelling-house in that building, or

(b) the tenancy is a tenancy for a term of years certain and is granted to a person who, immediately before it was granted, was the tenant under an earlier tenancy of that dwelling-house or any other dwelling-house in that building and, by virtue of this section, that earlier tenancy was not a protected tenancy,

and for the purposes of this subsection a tenancy shall be treated as being for a term of years certain notwithstanding that it is liable to determination by re-entry or on the happening of any event other than the giving of notice by the landlord to determine the term.

(6) For the purposes of this section a building is a purpose-built block of flats, if as constructed it contained, and it contains, two, or more flats; and for this purpose " flat " means a dwelling-house which—

(a) forms part only of a building; and

(b) is separated horizontally from another dwelling-house which forms part of the same building.

(7) For the purposes of this section, a person shall be treated as occupying a dwelling-house as his residence if, so far as the nature of the case allows, he fulfils the same conditions as, by virtue of section 3(2) above, are required to be fulfilled by a statutory tenant of a dwelling-house."

2. The following section shall be inserted after section 5 of the Rent (Scotland) Act 1971:—

" No protected tenancy where landlord's interest belongs to resident landlord.

5A.—(1) Subject to subsection (6) below, a tenancy of a dwelling-house which is granted on or after the commencement date within the meaning of the Rent Act 1974 shall not be a protected tenancy at any time if—

    (*a*) the dwelling-house forms part only of a building and that building is not a purpose-built block of flats; and

    (*b*) subject to subsection (2) below, the tenancy was granted by a person who, at the time when he granted it, occupied as his residence another dwelling-house which also forms part of that building; and

    (*c*) subject to subsection (3) below, at all times since the tenancy was granted, the interest of the landlord under the tenancy has belonged to a person who, at the time he owned that interest, occupied as his residence another dwelling-house which also formed part of that building.

(2) The condition in paragraph (*b*) of subsection (1) above shall be deemed to be fulfilled if the tenancy was granted by trustees and, at the time when the tenancy was granted, the interest of the landlord under the tenancy thereby created was held on trust for a person who was entitled to the liferent or to the fee or a share of the fee of that interest and who occupied as his residence a dwelling-house which forms part of the building referred to in paragraph (*a*) of that subsection.

(3) In determining whether the condition in paragraph (*c*) of subsection (1) above is at any time fulfilled with respect to a tenancy, there shall be disregarded—

    (*a*) any period of not more than 14 days beginning with the date of the conveyance of the interest of the landlord under the tenancy to an individual who, during that period, does not occupy as his residence another dwelling-house which forms part of the building concerned;

(b) if, within a period falling within paragraph (*a*) above, the individual concerned notifies the tenant in writing of his intention to occupy as his residence another such dwelling-house as is referred to in that paragraph, the period beginning with the date of the conveyance mentioned in that paragraph and ending—

    (i) at the expiry of the period of 6 months beginning on that date, or

    (ii) on the date on which the interest of the landlord under the tenancy ceases to be held by that individual, or

    (iii) on the date on which the condition in subsection (1)(*c*) above again applies,

whichever is the earlier; and

(*c*) any period of not more than 12 months beginning with the date of death of the landlord under the tenancy during which the interest of the landlord under the tenancy is vested in his executor.

(4) Throughout any period which, by virtue of subsection (3) above, falls to be disregarded for the purpose of determining whether the condition in subsection (1)(*c*) above is fulfilled with respect to a tenancy, no order for possession of the dwelling-house subject to that tenancy shall be made, other than an order which might be made if that tenancy were or, as the case may be, had been a regulated tenancy.

(5) During any period when—

(*a*) the interest of the landlord under the tenancy referred to in subsection (1) above is vested in trustees; and

(*b*) that interest is held on trust for a person who is entitled to the liferent or to the fee or a share of the fee of that interest and who occupies as his residence a dwelling-house forms part of the building referred to in paragraph (*a*) of that subsection,

the condition in paragraph (*c*) of that subsection shall be deemed to be fulfilled and, accordingly, no part of that period shall be disregarded by virtue of subsection (3) above.

(6) This section does not apply to a tenancy of a dwelling-house which forms part of a building if the tenancy is granted to a person who, immediately before it was granted, was a protected or statutory tenant of that dwelling-house or of any other dwelling-house in that building.

(7) For the purposes of this section, a person shall be treated as occupying a dwelling-house as his residence if, so far as the nature of the case allows, he would be regarded as retaining possession of the dwelling-house for the purposes of paragraph (*a*) of section 3(1) above if he were such a person as is referred to in that paragraph.

(8) For the purposes of this section—

(*a*) a building is a purpose-built block of flats if, as constructed it contained, and it contains, two or more flats, and for this purpose "flat" has the same meaning as in section 208(1) of the Housing (Scotland) Act 1966;

(*b*) " conveyance " includes the grant of a tenancy and any other conveyance or transfer other than upon death;

(*c*) " the date of the conveyance " means the date on which the conveyance was granted, delivered or otherwise made effective ".

PART II

AMENDMENTS OF PART IX OF RENT ACT 1968

3. In section 101 of the Rent Act 1968 (provisions where tenant shares accommodation with landlord) in paragraph (*c*) after the words " paragraph (*b*) above " there shall be inserted the words " or by reason of those circumstances and the operation of section 5A of this Act ".

4. After section 102 of that Act there shall be inserted the following section:—

" Application of Part VI to tenancies falling within section 5A.

102A.—(1) If and so long as a tenancy is, by virtue only of section 5A of this Act, precluded from being a protected tenancy, it shall be treated for the purposes of Part VI of this Act as a contract to which that Part applies, notwithstanding that the rent may not include payment for the use of furniture or for services.

(2) In any case where—

> (*a*) a tenancy which, by virtue only of section 5A of this Act, was precluded from being a protected tenancy ceases to be so precluded and accordingly become a protected tenancy, and
>
> (*b*) before it became a protected tenancy a rent was registered for the dwelling concerned under Part VI of this Act,

the amount which is so registered shall be deemed to be registered under Part IV of this Act as the rent for the dwelling-house which is let on that tenancy, and that registration shall be deemed to take effect on the day the tenancy becomes a protected tenancy.

(3) Section 44(3) of this Act shall not apply to an application for the registration under Part IV of this Act of a rent different from that which is deemed to be registered as mentioned in subsection (2) above.

(4) The reference in section 45(1)(*b*) of this Act to a rent being registered for a dwelling-house does not include a rent which is deemed to be registered as mentioned in subsection (2) above.

(5) If, immediately before a tenancy became a protected tenancy as mentioned in subsection (2)(*a*) above, the rates in respect of the dwelling concerned were borne as mentioned in subsection (2A) of section 74 of this Act and the fact that they were so borne was noted as required by that subsection, then, in the application of Part IV of this Act in relation to the protected tenancy, section 47(2) of this Act shall be deemed to apply.

(6) If, in a case where a tenancy becomes a protected tenancy as mentioned in subsection (2)(*a*) above,—

> (*a*) a notice to quit had been served in respect of the dwelling concerned before the date on which the tenancy became a protected tenancy, and
>
> (*b*) the period at the end of which that notice to quit takes effect had, before that date, been extended under Part VI of this Act, and
>
> (*c*) that period has not expired before that date,

the notice to quit shall take effect on the day following that date (whenever it would otherwise take effect) and, accordingly, on that day the protected tenancy shall become a statutory tenancy."

PART III

AMENDMENTS OF PART X OF RENT (SCOTLAND) ACT 1971

5. In section 118 of the Rent (Scotland) Act 1971 (provisions where tenant shares accommodation with landlord) in paragraph (*c*) after the words " paragraph (*b*) above " there shall be inserted the words " or by reason of those circumstances and the operation of section 5A of this Act ".

6. After section 119 of that Act there shall be inserted the following section:—

" Application of Part VII to tenancies falling within section 5A.

119A.—(1) If and so long as a tenancy is, by virtue only of section 5A of this Act, precluded from being a protected tenancy, it shall be treated for the purposes of Part VII of this Act as a contract to which that Part applies, notwithstanding that the rent may not include payment for the use of furniture or for services.

(2) In any case where—

    (*a*) a tenancy which, by virtue only of section 5A of this Act, was precluded from being a protected tenancy ceases to be so precluded and accordingly becomes a protected tenancy, and

    (*b*) before it became a protected tenancy a rent was registered for the dwelling-house concerned under Part VII of this Act,

the amount which is so registered shall be deemed to be registered under Part IV of this Act as the rent for the dwelling-house which is let on that tenancy, and that registration shall be deemed to take effect on the day the tenancy becomes a protected tenancy.

(3) Section 40(3) of this Act shall not apply to an application for the registration under Part IV of this Act of a rent different from that which is deemed to be registered as mentioned in subsection (2) above.

(4) The reference in section 41(1)(*b*) of this Act to a rent being registered for a dwelling-house does not include a rent which is deemed to be registered as mentioned in subsection (2) above.

(5) If, immediately before a tenancy became a protected tenancy as mentioned in subsection (2)(*a*) above, the rates in respect of the dwelling-house were

borne as mentioned in subsection (2A) of section 89 of this Act and the fact that they were so borne was noted as required by that subsection, then, in the application of Part IV of this Act in relation to the protected tenancy, section 43(2) of this Act shall be deemed to apply.

(6) If, in a case where a tenancy becomes a protected tenancy as mentioned in subsection (2)(*a*) above,—

(*a*) a notice to quit had been served in respect of the dwelling-house concerned before the date on which the tenancy became a protected tenancy, and

(*b*) the period at the end of which that notice to quit takes effect had, before that date, been extended under Part VII of this Act, and

(*c*) that period has not expired before that date,

the notice to quit shall take effect on the day following that date (whenever it would otherwise take effect) and, accordingly, on that day the protected tenancy shall become a statutory tenancy.''

SCHEDULE 3

Section 16(1).

TRANSITIONAL PROVISIONS

1.—(1) In any case where—

(a) before the commencement date a dwelling was subject to a tenancy which is a furnished letting, and

(b) the dwelling forms part only of a building, and that building is not a purpose-built block of flats within the meaning of section 5A of the Rent Act 1968, and

(c) on that date the interest of the lessor within the meaning of the relevant Part of the Rent Act, under the furnished letting—

  (i) belongs to a person who occupies as his residence another dwelling which also forms part of that building, or

  (ii) is vested in trustees as such and is or, if it is held on trust for sale, the proceeds of its sale are held on trust for a person who occupies as his residence another dwelling which also forms part of that building, and

(d) apart from this paragraph the furnished letting would, on the commencement date, become a protected furnished tenancy,

the Rent Act shall apply, subject to sub-paragraph (2) below, as if the tenancy had been granted on the commencement date and as if the condition in paragraph (b) of section 5A(1) of the Rent Act 1968 were fulfilled in relation to the grant of the tenancy.

(2) In the application of the Rent Act 1968 to a tenancy by virtue of this paragraph—

(a) subsection (5) of section 5A shall be omitted; and

(b) in section 102A any reference to section 5A of that Act shall be construed as including a reference to this paragraph.

(3) In any case where paragraphs (a), (b) and (d) of sub-paragraph (1) above apply but on the commencement date the interest referred to in paragraph (c) of that sub-paragraph is vested—

(a) in the personal representatives of a deceased person acting in that capacity, or

(b) by virtue of section 9 of the Administration of Estates Act 1925, in the Probate Judge, within the meaning of that Act, or

(c) in trustees as such,

then, if the deceased immediately before his death or, as the case may be, the settlor immediately before the creation of the trust occupied as his residence another dwelling which also formed part of the building referred to in paragraph (b) of sub-paragraph (1) above, that sub-paragraph shall apply as if the condition in paragraph (c) thereof were fulfilled.

(4) In the application of subsection (2)(c) of section 5A of the Rent Act 1968 in a case falling within sub-paragraph (3) above, any period before the commencement date during which the interest of the landlord is vested as mentioned in that subsection shall be disregarded in calculating the period of 12 months specified therein.

2.—(1) In any case where—

(a) before the commencement date a dwelling-house was subject to a tenancy which is a furnished letting; and

(b) the dwelling-house forms part only of a building and that building is not a purpose-built block of flats within the meaning of section 5A of the Act of 1971; and

(c) on that date the interest of the lessor, within the meaning of Part VII of that Act, under the furnished letting—

    (i) belongs to a person who occupies as his residence another dwelling-house which also forms part of that building, or

    (ii) is vested in trustees and is held on trust for a person who is entitled to the liferent or to the fee or a share of the fee of that interest and who occupies as his residence a dwelling-house which forms part of that building; and

(d) apart from this paragraph the furnished letting would, on the commencement date, become a protected furnished tenancy,

the Act of 1971 shall apply, subject to sub-paragraph (2) below, as if the tenancy had been granted on the commencement date and as if the condition in paragraph (b) of section 5A(1) of that Act were fulfilled in relation to the grant of the tenancy.

(2) In the application of the Act of 1971 to a tenancy by virtue of this paragraph—

(a) subsection (6) of section 5A shall be omitted; and

(b) in section 119A any reference to section 5A shall be construed as including a reference to this paragraph.

(3) In any case where paragraphs (*a*), (*b*) and (*d*) of sub-paragraph (1) above apply but on the commencement date the interest of the lessor under the furnished letting is vested in the executor of a deceased person, then, if that deceased person immediately before his death occupied as his residence another dwelling-house which also formed part of the building referred to in paragraph (*b*) of sub-paragraph (1) above, that sub-paragraph shall apply as if the condition in paragraph (*c*) thereof were fulfilled.

(4) In the application of subsection (3)(*c*) of section 5A of the Act of 1971, in a case falling within sub-paragraph (3) above, any period before the commencement date during which the interest of the lessor is vested in the executor as mentioned in that subsection shall be disregarded in calculating the period of 12 months specified in that subsection.

(5) In this paragraph " the Act of 1971 " means the Rent (Scotland) Act 1971.

3.—(1) This paragraph applies where the tenancy of a dwelling-house has come to an end before the commencement date and, if it had come to an end after that date, it would have then been a protected furnished tenancy.

(2) No order for possession of the dwelling-house shall be made which would not be made if the tenancy had been a protected furnished tenancy at the time it came to an end.

(3) Where a court has made an order for possession of the dwelling-house before the commencement date but the order has not been executed, the court, if of opinion that the order would not have been made if the tenancy had been a protected furnished tenancy when it came to an end, may, on the application of the person against whom it was made, rescind or vary it in such manner as the court thinks fit for the purpose of giving effect to section 1 of this Act.

(4) If the tenant under the tenancy which has come to an end duly retains possession of the dwelling-house on the commencement date without an order for possession having been made or after the rescission of such an order, he shall be deemed to do so as a statutory tenant under a regulated tenancy and, subject to sub-paragraph (8) below, as a person who became the statutory tenant on the termination of a protected tenancy under which he was the tenant; and, subject to sub-paragraphs (6) and (7) below, the tenancy referred to in sub-paragraph (1) above shall be treated, in relation to his statutory tenancy,—

> (*a*) as the original contract of tenancy for the purposes of section 12 of the Rent Act (terms and conditions of statutory tenancies); and

(*b*) as the previous contractual tenancy for the purposes of paragraph 2 of Part III of Schedule 3 to the Rent Act.

(5) In any case where—

    (*a*) immediately before the commencement date a rent is registered for a dwelling under the relevant Part of the Rent Act, and

    (*b*) on the commencement date a person becomes a statutory tenant of that dwelling by virtue of sub-paragraph (4) above,

the amount which is so registered under the relevant Part of the Rent Act shall be deemed to be registered under Part IV of that Act as the rent for that dwelling, and that registration shall be deemed to take effect on the commencement date.

(6) In England and Wales the High Court or the county court may by order vary all or any of the terms of the statutory tenancy imposed by sub-paragraph (4) above in any way appearing to the court to be just and equitable, and whether or not in a way authorised by the provisions of sections 23 and 24 of the Rent Act 1968.

(7) In Scotland the sheriff may by order vary all or any of the terms of the statutory tenancy imposed by sub-paragraph (4) above in any way appearing to him to be just and equitable, and whether or not in a way authorised by the provisions of sections 22 and 23 of the Rent (Scotland) Act 1971.

(8) If on the commencement date the dwelling-house is occupied by a person who would, if the tenancy had been a protected tenancy, have been the " first successor " as defined in paragraph 4 of Schedule 1 to the Rent Act—

    (*a*) an application under sub-paragraph (3) above may be made by that person, and

    (*b*) sub-paragraph (4) above shall apply where that person retains possession as it applies where the tenant retains possession, except that he shall be the first successor, as so defined.

4.—(1) The provisions of this paragraph shall have effect with respect to the period beginning on the commencement date and ending on the day appointed for the purposes of subsection (1) of section 11 of this Act, and in the following provisions of this paragraph that period is referred to as " the interim period ".

(2) During the interim period every allowance scheme (including an allowance scheme which is the model scheme, as defined in

section 20(7) of the Housing Finance Act 1972) shall be deemed to be varied to such extent as is necessary to take account of the provisions of subsections (2) to (5) of section 11 of this Act and of the repeals of provisions of Part II of that Act contained in Part I of Schedule 4 to this Act.

(3) No account shall be taken for the purposes of section 24 of the Housing Finance Act 1972 (publicity for schemes) of any deemed variation of a scheme which is effected by sub-paragraph (2) above.

(4) Where, during the interim period, an authority vary their allowance scheme to take account of the provisions of the sub-sections and of the repeals referred to in sub-paragraph (2) above, the variation shall not take effect until the day appointed as mentioned in sub-paragraph (1) above.

(5) At any time within the interim period an authority may vary their allowance scheme, with effect from the day appointed as mentioned in sub-paragraph (1) above, to take account of the modifications of Part II of the Housing Finance Act 1972 effected on and after that day by subsection (1) of section 11 of, and Part II of Schedule 4 to, this Act.

(6) In this paragraph " allowance scheme " and " authority " have the same meanings as in Part II of the Housing Finance Act 1972.

5. Subsection (3) of section 20 of the Housing Finance Act 1972 (proposals for regulations varying Schedules 3 and 4 to that Act to be referred to the Advisory Committee on Rent Rebates and Rent Allowances) shall not apply to regulations which are—

(a) made within the period of three months beginning on the commencement date; and

(b) expressed to be made for the purpose of making in either of those Schedules variations consequential upon provision made by virtue of paragraph (c) of section 25(3) of that Act (as set out in section 11 (7) of this Act).

6.—(1) The provisions of this paragraph shall have effect with respect to the period beginning on the commencement date and ending on the day appointed for the purposes of subsection (1) of section 12 of this Act, and in the following provisions of this paragraph that period is referred to as " the interim period".

(2) During the interim period every allowance scheme (including an allowance scheme which is the model scheme as defined in section 17(5) of the Act of 1972) shall be deemed to be varied to such extent as is necessary to take account of the provisions of sub-sections (2) to (4) of section 12 of this Act.

(3) No account shall be taken for the purposes of section 19(2) of the Act of 1972 (publicity for allowance schemes) of any deemed variation of a scheme which is effected by sub-paragraph (2) above.

(4) Where, during the interim period, an authority vary their allowance scheme to take account of the provisions of the sub-sections referred to in sub-paragraph (2) above, the variation shall not take effect until the day appointed as mentioned in sub-paragraph (1) above.

(5) At any time within the interim period an authority may vary, with effect from the day appointed as mentioned in sub-paragraph (1) above, their allowance scheme to take account of the modifications of section 16 of the Act of 1972 effected on and after that day by subsection (1) of section 12 of this Act.

(6) In this paragraph " the Act of 1972 " means the Housing (Financial Provisions) (Scotland) Act 1972; and " allowance scheme " and " authority " have the same meanings as in Part II of the Act of 1972.

SCHEDULE 4

ENACTMENTS REPEALED
PART I
REPEALS TAKING EFFECT ON COMMENCEMENT

Chapter	Short Title	Extent of Repeal
1968 c. 23.	The Rent Act 1968.	In section 2(3) the words " or the use of furniture ", " or use of furniture " and " or the use ". Section 73(3). In section 75, in subsection (1) the words " on the ground of change of circumstances " and subsection (2). Section 78(1)(c). In Schedule 3, in Case 9, the word " also ". In Schedule 7, in paragraph 1 the word " and " at the end of sub-paragraph (b).
1971 c. 28.	The Rent (Scotland) Act 1971.	In section 2(3) the words " or the use of furniture ", " or use of furniture " and " or the use ". In section 88(3) the words " or this section as extended by section 90 below ". In section 89(2) the words " or that section as extended by section 90 below ". In section 90, in subsection (1) the words " on the ground of change of circumstances " and subsection (2). Section 93(1)(c). In Schedule 3, in Case 9, the word " also ". In Schedule 7, in paragraph 1 the word " and " at the end of sub-paragraph (b).
1972 c. 46.	The Housing (Financial Provisions) (Scotland) Act 1972.	In Schedule 3, in paragraph 15(1)(g)(ii) the words " 125 per cent. of ".
1972 c. 47.	The Housing Finance Act 1972.	In section 23, in subsection (1) the words " or making orders under section 25(3A) of this Act ". In section 25, in subsection (1) the proviso, subsection (3A) and in subsection (4) the words " and orders ". Section 89.
1973 c. 6.	The Furnished Lettings (Rent Allowances) Act 1973.	In Schedule 1, paragraphs 17, 19 and 20.

PART II

REPEALS TAKING EFFECT ON DAY APPOINTED UNDER SUBSECTION (1) OF SECTIONS 11 AND 12

Chapter	Short Title	Extent of Repeal
1972 c. 46.	The Housing (Financial Provisions) (Scotland) Act 1972.	In section 16, in subsections (3), (5) and (7) the words " being a qualified person within the meaning of sub-section (8) of this section ", and subsections (8), (9) and (10).
1972 c. 47.	The Housing Finance Act 1972.	In section 19, in subsections (4) and (6) the words " being a qualified person within the meaning of sub-section (12) below ", in subsection (8A), paragraph (b) and the word " and " immediately preceding it and subsections (12) to (14). In section 23, in subsection (1) the words from " or to the descriptions " to the end of the sub-section. In section 24, in subsection (10) the words from " or to a person " to " would be a private tenant " and in subsection (11) the words from " or for a person " to " would be a private tenant of a dwelling ".
1973 c. 6.	The Furnished Lettings (Rent Allowances) Act 1973.	In Schedule 1, paragraphs 10 and 12.